MINDSCIENCE

MindScience

AN EAST-WEST DIALOGUE

The Dalai Lama
Herbert Benson • Robert A. F. Thurman
Daniel Goleman • Howard Gardner
et alii

*Proceedings of a symposium sponsored by
the Mind/Body Medical Institute of
Harvard Medical School & New England Deaconess Hospital,
and
Tibet House New York*

Edited by
Daniel Goleman & Robert A. F. Thurman

WISDOM PUBLICATIONS
Boston

First published 1991

WISDOM PUBLICATIONS
361 Newbury Street
Boston, MA 02115

Library of Congress Cataloging in Publication Data

MindScience: An East-West Dialogue
His Holiness the Dalai Lama et al.
edited by Daniel Goleman and Robert Thurman.
p. cm.
Talks delivered on March 24, 1991 at a symposium called
Mind Science,
part of the continuing education program of Harvard Medical School.
Includes bibliographical references and index.
ISBN 0 86171 066 5
1. Buddhism—Psychology—Congresses.
2. Meditation—Physiological aspects—Congresses.
3. Meditation—Buddhism—Congresses.
I. Bstan-'dzin-rgya-mtsho, Dalai Lama XIV, 1935–.
II. Goleman, Daniel. III. Thurman, Robert A. F.
IV. Harvard Medical School.
BQ4570. P76M57 1991 294.3'375—dc20 91-30288

Manufactured in the United States of America.

Contents

THE DALAI LAMA

Foreword

I believe the ultimate aim of all human beings is to obtain happiness and a sense of fulfillment. These objectives can be achieved through physical amenities and proper mental development, but the dominant and ultimate factor is the mental aspect. In order to achieve these objectives one must have knowledge about both mind and matter.

Science has made tremendous progress in understanding and harnessing matter. Buddhism, on the other hand, has a profound philosophy and over the centuries has developed a systematic method of shaping and developing the mind. Whether we are scientists or spiritual practitioners our basic needs and aspirations are the same. Scientists may study mainly matter but they cannot ignore the human mind, or consciousness; spiritual practitioners may be engaging mainly in developing the mind but they cannot completely ignore their physical needs. It is for this reason that I have always stressed the importance of combining both the mental and the material approach to achieving happiness for humankind. I am therefore very happy to learn that Wisdom is publishing this book *MindScience*.

August 5, 1991

Preface

The talks published here were originally delivered at a symposium called *Mind Science: A Dialogue between East and West*. Part of a program of Harvard Medical School's Department of Continuing Medical Education, the symposium took place on March 24, 1991, at the Kresge Auditorium, Massachusetts Institute of Technology, Cambridge, under the joint auspices of the Mind/Body Medical Institute and Tibet House New York. It gathered together experts from the fields of medicine, psychiatry, psychobiology, neurobiology, education, comparative religion and Indo-Tibetan Buddhism in open dialogue and exchange on the various concepts, approaches and understandings, East and West, of the science of mind. Guest of honor was His Holiness the Dalai Lama, the Nobel Peace Prize Laureate.

The symposium celebrated more than a decade of collaborative research between the Tibetan Buddhist community and Harvard Medical School. This work had its genesis on October 18, 1979, when I met with His Holiness the Dalai Lama during his first visit to Harvard University. On this occasion, I had explained our laboratory's experiments on the physiological effects of simple meditative techniques, and requested permission to study several of the advanced meditative techniques of Tibetan Buddhism.

The rationale was straightforward: If simple meditative techniques resulted in such notable physiological changes as decreased metabolism, heart rate, blood pressure and rate of breathing, as well as distinctive brainwave patterns, what could the effects of advanced meditative techniques be? Could they possibly demonstrate even more striking mind/body interactions? We had been attempting to investigate these advanced techniques for several years, but could find no practitioners who would consent to be studied—they had little interest in the scientific documentation of their practices.

I had just finished reading Alexandra David-Neel's *Magic and Mystery of Tibet,* which contained her early-twentieth-century accounts of *gTum-mo* yoga being performed by Tibetan Buddhist monks. In this practice, an internal heat, which is generated for religious purposes, has demonstrable effects on the body. David-Neel described what she saw in a midwinter encounter:

> The neophytes sit on the ground, cross-legged and naked. Sheets are dipped in the icy water, each man wraps himself in one of them and must dry it on his body. As soon as the sheet has become dry, it is again dipped in the water and placed on the novice's body to be dried as before. The operation goes on [in] that fashion until daybreak. Then he who has dried the largest number of sheets is acknowledged the winner of the competition.
>
> Besides drying wet sheets on one's body, there exist various other tests to ascertain the degree of heat which the neophyte is able to radiate. One of these tests consists in sitting in the snow. The quantity of snow melted under the man and the distance at which it melts around him are taken as measures of his ability.[1]

I hoped that with the permission of His Holiness the Dalai Lama, I would be allowed access to study the remarkable alleged mind/body effects of *gTum-mo.*

Our October 1979 meeting took place in the living room of the Dana-Palmer House in Cambridge, an 1823 building in which William James had lived and where he is believed to have conceived his idea of a pluralistic universe. After I had explained my rationale for requesting to study practitioners of *gTum-mo,* His Holiness replied, 'It will be very difficult to measure these abilities. The people who practice this meditation do so for religious purposes. It must be experienced in order to feel the benefits. You *must* experience it first.' Then he added, 'Still, our culture is undergoing many changes. We have been forced out of our homeland into exile . . . perhaps there is some worth in allowing this study to be done.'

Several months later I received a letter from His Holiness's office inviting us to study three *gTum-mo* practitioners who lived near Dharamsala, India. Some of the successful and striking results of these studies and others are described in this book. We determined through scientifically-based investigations that advanced meditative techniques do indeed lead to profound, hitherto unrecognized human mind/body capacities.

In the autumn of 1990, we believed that it was time to take stock of where these experiments had brought us, and thus the Mind Science Symposium was conceived. His Holiness agreed to attend, and the dialogue was further expanded to embrace Eastern and Western concepts of the mind.

I am grateful to all those who attended and made the symposium such a success. My hope is that it will not only act as a watershed for the decade of fruitful mind science interactions between East and West, but also point to future advances in our continuing collaboration.

HERBERT BENSON, MD
Boston, 1991

Introduction

A Western Perspective

It was the historian Arnold Toynbee who predicted that one of the most significant events of the twentieth century would be the coming of Buddhism to the West. For modern psychology, that may be so in a special sense: as a discipline we are awakening to the fact that there is a more ancient science of mind, and perhaps a wiser one, than our own, and that its fullest articulation is in Buddhism.

Modern psychology has had a myopic historical vision, assuming that the psychological endeavor began in Europe and America within the last century or so. We have lost sight of the deeper roots of our discipline in philosophy, and, in turn, of philosophy in religion. Few psychologists, for example, remember that William James, one of the fathers of modern psychology, was a member of the philosophy department at Harvard until he founded the psychology department there near the turn of the century.

But Buddhism confronts modern psychology with two facts: that the systematic study of the mind and its workings dates back to well before the Christian era, and that this exploration is at the heart of spiritual life. Indeed, every major world religion harbors an esoteric psychology, a science of mind, usually little known to its lay practitioners. In Islam, for instance, it is to be found in Sufism; in Judaism, in the kabbalah; in Christianity, in monastic meditation manuals.

In Buddhism, the classical mind science is called 'Abhidharma'. Developed, systematized and refined over the thousand years after Gautama Buddha's teaching in the fifth century BCE, Abhidharma is an elaborate model of the mind. Like any thorough psychological system, it describes in detail the workings of perception, cognition, affect and motivation. A dynamic model, Abhidharma analyzes both the roots of human suffering and a way out of that suffering—the central message of Buddhism cast in the technical language of a psychology.

Apart from the metaphysical context of Abhidharma, it represents a significant entity from the perspective of modern psychology: It is a psychological system with completely different roots. As such, for the first time it offers modern psychology something akin to a 'close encounter of the third kind'—a meeting with an alien intelligence that few, if any, really thought existed. Certainly, most psychologists and psychiatrists, if asked, would have said that there is no other fully mature psychology beyond the fold of modern Western thought. Now, though, it is clear that there is one, and that it has something of significance to say to the psychologies of the West.

Buddhist psychology offers modern psychology the opportunity for genuine dialogue with a system of thought that has evolved outside the conceptual systems that have spawned contemporary psychology. Here is a fully-realized psychology that offers the chance for a complementary view of many of the fundamental issues of modern psychology: the nature of mind; the limits of human potential for growth; the possibilities for mental health; the means for psychological change and transformation.

This symposium marks a beginning of that dialogue. As it continues, Western psychologists will discover that, just as there are many schools of thought in Western psychology, there is an equally diverse range of schools within Buddhist psychology—Abhidharma is the classical Buddhist psychology, but there are several versions of it by now. And, especially within Tibetan Buddhism, there are many more psychological systems, each elaborating its own practical applications in psychospiritual development.

The structure of this book follows the order of the symposium, its two parts marking the division between the morning and afternoon sessions.

In Chapter One, His Holiness the Dalai Lama describes the Buddhist concept of mind, bridging the views of scientific materialism and religion. He points out that understanding the nature of mind is fundamental to Buddhist thought. Tibetan teachings include a detailed map of how changes in the mind and body affect each other, and techniques for bringing those affects under voluntary control. The Tibetan view of the subtle relationships between mind and body holds that it is possible to separate mind from body—one of many notions that can be tested by researchers as their studies enrich our understanding of mind/body links.

In the dialogue with neuroscientists that follows in Chapter Two, His Holiness addresses several issues that are particularly challenging to Western science. These include whether or not mind can observe and understand its own nature; similarities between mathematical lawfulness of occurrences and the workings of karma; the Buddhist concept of emptiness and the ultimate nature of mind; the roots of psychological confusion and disturbances. Also explored is the question of gross and subtle levels of mind, and the provocative possibility that a subtle level of mind might exist independent of body.

Dr. Herbert Benson, in Chapter Three, reviews his pioneering research on the mind/body relationship, and especially on the 'relaxation response', which combines ancient meditation techniques with modern medicine. He also describes his more recent work in which advanced Tibetan meditators were studied practicing *gTum-mo* yoga and striking changes in oxygen consumption and body temperature were found. Such work, he hopes, can increase our understanding of how the mind can influence the body.

In Chapter Four, Robert Thurman addresses the question as to what Western cognitive science and neuroscience stand to gain from Tibetan mind science. He traces the development of Buddhist mind science, arguing for its pressing relevance by making the point that in the West our power to affect outer reality has far outstripped our power over ourselves. In suggesting what Tibetan mind science has to offer he cites as an example the remarkable diagnostic abilities of those trained in the Tibetan medicine method of pulse-taking. And he describes the inner states of the *gTum-mo* practitioner—the inner technology that creates the changes Dr. Benson has measured.

Howard Gardner's topic in Chapter Five is the modern Western view of the mind as found in cognitive science. His focus is on *hard* cognition: thinking, intelligence, rationality—as opposed to feeling, spirit and consciousness. And his plea is that we make use of all the disciplines and experience available—'what is in the East as well as what is in the West'—in a spirit of ecumenicism in which each system mutually shapes the understanding of the other. He proposes a genuine dialogue, with a promise of a final synthesis greater than where each began.

In Chapter Six, I compare Tibetan and Western models of mental health. Like Western psychology, the Tibetan system offers a model of the mind and its workings, as well as a definition of mental health and a way to achieve it. But the vision of human possibilities in the Tibetan model holds forth a model of mental well being that offers a challenge to the paradigms of Western perspective psychology: it asserts that cessation of the suffering caused by clinging and anger and the attainment of states such as equanimity and compassion are not just desirable but possible.

Finally, in the concluding panel discussion in Chapter Seven, several of the issues raised in the symposium are further discussed and elaborated upon, particularly some that suggest a fertile meeting point between the psychologies of East and West.

For me, this dialogue under the auspices of Harvard Medical School marks a full circle in a personal journey. I first encountered Abhidharma—and Tibetan Buddhism—in 1970, while on a Harvard Predoctoral Travelling Fellowship in India. I was fascinated: here was a psychological system with a radically different set of premises from any to which I had previously been exposed. It was a system that not only explained how the mind worked, but how it could be methodically transformed. And it was a psychology that held out as the ideal of human development spiritual values like equanimity and compassion—a vision far more hopeful than that of any modern psychology.

On my return to Harvard I found the beginnings of research into meditation, the applied technology of Buddhist and other Eastern psychologies. At the Medical School, Herbert Benson was engaged in his pioneering work on the relaxation response; in my own department of psychology, Gary Schwartz, Richard Davidson and I began a similar program of research on meditation.

While the fruits of research on meditation for behavioral medicine have been great, this dialogue represents a next stage. Meditation is but one of many applied tools from the psychologies of the East. As we explore what else of value for modern life is to be found from that source, we may discover that there are yet more things in heaven and earth than are dreamt of in our psychology.

DANIEL GOLEMAN

A Tibetan Perspective

Tibet has the inner science civilization *par excellence*. In her mountain remoteness, her finest minds developed and refined the inner sciences received from the rich and ancient Indian Buddhist civilization. The monastic universities in which Tibetans lived and worked, some with over ten thousand scholars resident, were utterly dedicated to a curriculum that centered on these inner sciences. And the entire Tibetan nation was utterly dedicated to the flourishing of those monastic universities.

Bertrand Russell once said that each of the three great philosophical civilizations, the Western, the Chinese and the Indian, had its own specialty. The Western excelled in exploring the relationship between humanity and nature, and so developed the extraordinary sciences of the material universe. The Chinese excelled in exploring the relationships within society, and so developed a remarkably peaceful history and an elegant civilization, presently challenged by the difficult encounter with modernity. But the Indian excelled in exploring the human's inner world, and so developed the supreme knowledge of the self, its depth consciousness, its processes of knowing and expressing, and its extraordinary states.

Over a period of millennia, the Indian Buddhist civilization profoundly influenced all the other civilizations of Asia. Eventually Buddhism was lost in India, and the twentieth century has seen its disappearance from much of the rest of Asia, as well. But in the seventh century CE, the Tibetan civilization opened itself in a unique way to receive the great treasures of Indian Buddhism and, over the next thirteen centuries, the Tibetan people became more and more devoted to it, as it transformed their lives, land, society and deepest hearts.

The Tibetans' greatest gifts to the world today are their knowledge of these matchless inner sciences and their mastery of the rich panoply of the arts of transformation of the human mind that derive from these inner sciences. Although the West appreciates other cultures for various excellences and exotic beauties, such as their spiritual treasures or works of art, it tends to consider itself the dominant intellect on the planet because of its mastery over the material universe.

But this might be a logical error. Perhaps those who choose *not* to develop such power over external nature understand it best. Perhaps those who make it a priority to understand themselves and control their own minds and actions have the superior intellects. Perhaps we in the West have something *scientific* to learn from them.

The Mind Science Symposium had an atmosphere of inspiration and delight for all concerned, because it was grounded on mutual respect. Westerners as well as Easterners were open to the possibility that they could learn from each other.

Tibet House New York was established in 1987 to help preserve Tibetan civilization, which has been threatened by the most devastating kind of encounter with modernity—military occupation and industrial colonization. While the world of officialdom tries not to recognize the suffering of Tibet and her people, a grass-roots movement from thirty-seven countries proclaimed 1991 to be the International Year of Tibet. It is altogether fitting and deeply moving that the intellectual jewel of Tibet, the healing medicine of Tibet, the unique gift of Tibet—its inner arts and sciences—should have been celebrated at the very beginning of the International Year. I am grateful to Herbert Benson and his colleagues at the Mind/Body Medical Institute for working with Tibet House to honor Tibetan civilization and its ancient tradition of inner science in this way.

Around 1,350 years ago, Tibet was a great military empire in the heart of Asia. But her emperors eventually tired of war and conquest and invited the inner scientists of India to establish their teachings and institutions in Tibet. They thus began the long transformation of Tibet from a culture of violence that held the conquest of others to be the highest goal, to a civilization of nonviolence where the conquest of self was the highest goal. It is my hope that the inner science conferences and studies of the past decade and the ongoing work of the future will all contribute to the world becoming a more peaceful place.

ROBERT A. F. THURMAN

PART ONE

BUDDHISM, NEUROSCIENCE &
THE MEDICAL SCIENCES

I

The Buddhist Concept of Mind

The Dalai Lama
Nobel Peace Prize Laureate

Translated by Geshe Thubten Jinpa

The Buddhist Concept of Mind

I would like to explain briefly the basic Buddhist concept of mind and some of the techniques employed in Buddhism for training the mind. The primary aim of these techniques is the attainment of enlightenment, but it is possible to experience even mundane benefits, such as good health, by practicing them.

As a result of meeting with people from different religious and cultural backgrounds, including scientists and radical materialists, I discovered that there are some people who do not even accept the existence of mind. This led me to believe that Buddhism could serve as a bridge between radical materialism and religion, because Buddhism is accepted as belonging to neither camp. From the radical materialists' viewpoint, Buddhism is an ideology that accepts the existence of mind, and is thus a faith-oriented system like other religions. However, since Buddhism does not accept the concept of a Creator God but emphasizes instead self-reliance and the individual's own power and potential, other religions regard Buddhism as a kind of atheism. Since neither side accepts Buddhism as belonging to its own camp, this gives Buddhists the opportunity to build a bridge between the two.

First of all, I would like to give a brief account of the general approach of Buddhist thought and practice common to both the Theravada and Mahayana traditions of Buddhism.

One very obvious feature in Buddhism is the element of faith and devotion. This is particularly apparent in the practice known as 'taking refuge in the three jewels':[2] the Buddha, Dharma and Sangha. To understand the role that faith and devotion play in this practice, emphasis is placed on clearly understanding the nature of the path in which one is taking refuge, called Dharma or the 'Way' by the Buddha.

The emphasis on first understanding the nature of the path, or

Dharma, can be appreciated by considering how we normally relate
to someone whom we take to be a great authority on a particular
subject. We do not regard a person as an authority simply on the basis
of their fame, position, power, good looks, wealth and so on, but
rather because we find what they say on issues related to their
particular field of expertise convincing and reliable. In brief, we do
not generally take a person to be an authority on a subject simply out
of respect and admiration for them as a person.

Similarly, in Buddhism, when we take the Buddha as an authority,
as a reliable teacher, we do so on the basis of having investigated and
examined his principal teaching, the Four Noble Truths.3 It is only
after having investigated the validity and reliability of this doctrine
that we accept the Buddha, who propounded it, as a reliable guide.

In order to understand the profound aspects of the Four Noble
Truths, the principal doctrine of Buddhism, it is crucial to understand
what are known as the 'two truths'.4 The two truths refer to the
fundamental Buddhist philosophical view that there are two levels of
reality. One level is the empirical, phenomenal and relative level that
appears to us, where functions such as causes and conditions, names
and labels, and so on can be validly understood. The other is a deeper
level of existence beyond that, which Buddhist philosophers describe
as the fundamental, or ultimate, nature of reality, and which is often
technically referred to as 'emptiness'.

When investigating the ultimate nature of reality, Buddhist
thinkers take the Buddha's words not so much as an ultimate authority, but rather as a key to assist their own insight; for the ultimate
authority must always rest with the individual's own reason and
critical analysis. This is why we find various conceptions of reality in
Buddhist literature. Each is based on a different level of understanding of the ultimate nature.

In the sutras, the collected original teachings of the Buddha, the
Buddha himself states that his words are not to be accepted as valid
simply out of respect and reverence for him, but rather should be
examined just as a goldsmith would test the purity and quality of gold
that he wished to purchase by subjecting it to various types of
examination.5 Similarly, we should examine the words of the Buddha,
and if we find them to be reliable and convincing through our own
reasoning and understanding, we should accept them as valid.

Another area in which we find the element of faith and devotion playing an obvious and crucial role is in the practice of Buddhist tantra. But even here, careful examination will show that the entire system of tantric practice is based upon an understanding of the ultimate nature of reality. Without this, one cannot even begin a genuine practice of tantra. So, in essence, reason and understanding are fundamental to the Buddhist approach on both the theoretical and the practical levels.

One of the fundamental views in Buddhism is the principle of 'dependent origination'. This states that all phenomena, both subjective experiences and external objects, come into existence in dependence upon causes and conditions; nothing comes into existence uncaused. Given this principle, it becomes crucial to understand what causality is and what types of cause there are. In Buddhist literature, two main categories of causation are mentioned: (i) external causes in the form of physical objects and events, and (ii) internal causes such as cognitive and mental events.

The reason for an understanding of causality being so important in Buddhist thought and practice is that it relates directly to sentient beings' feelings of pain and pleasure and the other experiences that dominate their lives, which arise not only from internal mechanisms but also from external causes and conditions. Therefore it is crucial to understand not only the internal workings of mental and cognitive causation but also their relationship to the external material world.

The fact that our inner experiences of pleasure and pain are in the nature of subjective mental and cognitive states is very obvious to us. But how those inner subjective events relate to external circumstances and the material world poses a critical problem. The question of whether there is an external physical reality independent of sentient beings' consciousness and mind has been extensively discussed by Buddhist thinkers. Naturally, there are divergent views on this issue among the various philosophical schools of thought. One such school[6] asserts that there is no external reality, not even external objects, and that the material world we perceive is in essence merely a projection of our minds. From many points of view, this conclusion is rather extreme. Philosophically, and for that matter conceptually, it seems more coherent to maintain a position that accepts the reality not only of the subjective world of the mind but also of the external objects of the physical world.

Now, if we examine the origins of our inner experiences and of external matter, we find that there is a fundamental uniformity in the nature of their existence in that both are governed by the principle of causality. Just as in the inner world of mental and cognitive events every moment of experience comes from its preceding continuum and so on *ad infinitum*, similarly in the physical world every object and event must have a preceding continuum that serves as its cause, from which the present moment of external matter comes into existence.

In some Buddhist literature, we find that in terms of the origin of its continuum, the macroscopic world of our physical reality can be traced back finally to an original state in which all material particles are condensed into what are known as 'space particles'.7 If all the physical matter of our macroscopic universe can be traced to such an original state, the question then arises as to how these particles later interact with each other and evolve into a macroscopic world that can have direct bearing on sentient beings' inner experiences of pleasure and pain. To answer this, Buddhists turn to the doctrine of karma, the invisible workings of actions and their effects, which provides an explanation as to how these inanimate space particles evolve into various manifestations.

The invisible workings of actions, or karmic force (*karma* means action), are intimately linked to the motivation in the human mind that gives rise to these actions. Therefore an understanding of the nature of mind and its role is crucial to an understanding of human experience and the relationship between mind and matter. We can see from our own experience that our state of mind plays a major role in our day-to-day experience and physical and mental well-being. If a person has a calm and stable mind, this influences his or her attitude and behavior in relation to others. In other words, if someone remains in a state of mind that is calm, tranquil and peaceful, external surroundings or conditions can cause them only limited disturbance. But it is extremely difficult for someone whose mental state is restless to be calm or joyful even when they are surrounded by the best facilities and the best of friends. This indicates that our mental attitude is a critical factor in determining our experience of joy and happiness, and thus also our good health.

To sum up, there are two reasons why it is important to understand the nature of mind. One is because there is an intimate connection between mind and karma. The other is that our state of mind plays a crucial role in our experience of happiness and suffering. If understanding the mind is very important, what then is mind, and what is its nature?

Buddhist literature, both sutra and tantra, contains extensive discussions on mind and its nature. Tantra, in particular, discusses the various levels of subtlety of mind and consciousness. The sutras do not talk much about the relationship between the various states of mind and their corresponding physiological states. Tantric literature, on the other hand, is replete with references to the various subtleties of the levels of consciousness and their relationship to such physiological states as the vital energy centers within the body, the energy channels, the energies that flow within these and so on. The tantras also explain how, by manipulating the various physiological factors through specific meditative yogic practices, one can effect various states of consciousness.[8]

According to tantra, the ultimate nature of mind is essentially pure. This pristine nature is technically called 'clear light'. The various afflictive emotions such as desire, hatred and jealousy are products of conditioning. They are not intrinsic qualities of the mind because the mind can be cleansed of them. When this clear light nature of mind is veiled or inhibited from expressing its true essence by the conditioning of the afflictive emotions and thoughts, the person is said to be caught in the cycle of existence, samsara. But when, by applying appropriate meditative techniques and practices, the individual is able to fully experience this clear light nature of mind free from the influence and conditioning of the afflictive states, he or she is on the way to true liberation and full enlightenment.

Hence, from the Buddhist point of view, both bondage and true freedom depend on the varying states of this clear light mind, and the resultant state that meditators try to attain through the application of various meditative techniques is one in which this ultimate nature of mind fully manifests all its positive potential, enlightenment, or Buddhahood. An understanding of the clear light mind therefore becomes crucial in the context of spiritual endeavor.

In our own day-to-day experiences we can observe that, especially on the gross level, our mind is interrelated with and dependent upon the physiological states of the body. Just as our state of mind, be it depressed or joyful, affects our physical health, so too does our physical state affect our mind. As I mentioned earlier, Buddhist tantric literature mentions specific energy centers within the body that may, I think, have some connection with what some neurobiologists call the second brain, the immune system. These energy centers play a crucial role in increasing or decreasing the various emotional states within our mind. It is because of the intimate relationship between mind and body and the existence of these special physiological centers within our body that physical yoga exercises and the application of special meditative techniques aimed at training the mind can have positive effects on health. It has been shown, for example, that by applying appropriate meditative techniques, we can control our respiration and increase or decrease our body temperature.[9]

Furthermore, just as we can apply various meditative techniques during the waking state, so too, on the basis of understanding the subtle relationship between mind and body, can we practice various meditations while we are in dream states. The implication of the potential of such practices is that at a certain level it is possible to separate the gross levels of consciousness from gross physical states and arrive at a subtler level of mind and body. In other words, you can separate your mind from your coarse physical body. You could, for example, separate your mind from your body during sleep and do some extra work that you cannot do in your ordinary body. However, you might not get paid for it!

So you can see here the clear indication of a close link between body and mind: they can be complementary. In light of this, I am very glad to see that some scientists are undertaking significant research in the mind/body relationship and its implications for our understanding of the nature of mental and physical well-being. My old friend Dr. Benson, for example, has been carrying out experiments on Tibetan Buddhist meditators for some years now. Similar research work is also being undertaken in Czechoslovakia. Judging by our findings so far, I feel confident that there is still a great deal to be done in the future.

As the insights we gain from such research grow, there is no doubt that our understanding of mind and body, and also of physical and mental health, will be greatly enriched. Some modern scholars describe Buddhism not as a religion but as a science of mind, and there seem to be some grounds for this claim.

Dialogue:
Buddhism, Neuroscience & the
Medical Sciences

The Dalai Lama
Nobel Peace Prize Laureate

David M. Bear, MD
Professor of Psychiatry,
University of Massachusetts Medical Center

Geshe Thubten Jinpa
Translator

Herbert Benson, MD
Associate Professor of Medicine, Harvard Medical School;
President, Mind/Body Medical Institute

Steven W. Matthysse, Ph.D
Associate Professor of Psychobiology, Harvard Medical School;
Psychobiologist, McLean Hospital

David D. Potter, MD
Robert Winthrop Professor of Neurobiology, Harvard Medical School

Joseph J. Schildkraut, MD
Professor of Psychiatry, Harvard Medical School

Carl E. Schwartz, MD
Instructor in Psychiatry, Harvard Medical School

Dialogue:
Buddhism, Neuroscience & the
Medical Sciences

SCHILDKRAUT: I would like to begin by asking Your Holiness to speak to us more about the nature of mind, its coarse nature as well as its more subtle nature. And as you are doing this, perhaps you could address the question, 'How can mind observe and understand the nature of mind?', that is, 'How can mind study itself?'

DALAI LAMA: In general, the mind can be defined as an entity that has the nature of mere experience, that is, 'clarity and knowing'. It is the knowing nature, or agency, that is called mind, and this is non-material. But within the category of mind there are also gross levels, such as our sensory perceptions, which cannot function or even come into being without depending on physical organs like our senses. And within the category of the sixth consciousness, the mental consciousness,[10] there are various divisions, or types, of mental consciousness that are heavily dependent upon the physiological basis, our brain, for their arising. These types of mind cannot be understood in isolation from their physiological bases.

Now a crucial question arises: How is it that these various types of cognitive events—the sensory perceptions, mental states and so forth—can exist and possess this nature of knowing, luminosity and clarity? According to the Buddhist science of mind, these cognitive events possess the nature of knowing because of the fundamental nature of clarity that underlies all cognitive events. This is what I described earlier as the mind's fundamental nature, the clear light nature of mind. Therefore, when various mental states are described in Buddhist literature, you will find discussions of the different types of conditions that give rise to cognitive events. For example, in the case of sensory perceptions, external objects serve as the objective, or causal, condition; the immediately preceding moment of consciousness is the immediate condition; and the sense organ is the

physiological or dominant condition. It is on the basis of the aggrega-
tion of these three conditions—causal, immediate and physiological—that experiences such as sensory perceptions occur.

Another distinctive feature of mind is that it has the capacity to
observe itself. The issue of mind's ability to observe and examine itself
has long been an important philosophical question. In general, there
are different ways in which mind can observe itself. For instance, in
the case of examining a past experience, such as things that happened
yesterday, you recall that experience and examine your memory of it,
so the problem does not arise. But we also have experiences during
which the observing mind becomes aware of itself while still engaged
in its observed experience. Here, because both observing mind and
observed mental states are present at the same time, we cannot
explain the phenomenon of the mind becoming self-aware, being
subject and object simultaneously, through appealing to the factor of
time lapse.

Thus it is important to understand that when we talk about mind,
we are talking about a highly intricate network of different mental
events and states. Through the introspective properties of mind we
can observe, for example, what specific thoughts are in our mind at a
given moment, what objects our minds are holding, what kinds of
intentions we have and so on. In a meditative state, for example,
when you are meditating and cultivating a single-pointedness of
mind, you constantly apply the introspective faculty to analyze
whether or not your mental attention is single-pointedly focused on
the object, whether there is any laxity involved, whether you are
distracted and so forth. In this situation you are applying various
mental factors and it is not as if a single mind were examining itself.
Rather, you are applying various different types of mental factor to
examine your mind.

As to the question of whether or not a single mental state can
observe and examine itself, this has been a very important and difficult question in the Buddhist science of mind. Some Buddhist
thinkers have maintained that there is a faculty of mind called 'self-
consciousness', or 'self-awareness'. It could be said that this is an
apperceptive faculty of mind, one that can observe itself. But this
contention has been disputed. Those who maintain that such an
apperceptive faculty exists distinguish two aspects within the mental,
or cognitive, event. One of these is external and object-oriented in the

sense that there is a duality of subject and object, while the other is introspective in nature and it is this that enables the mind to observe itself. The existence of this apperceptive self-cognizing faculty of mind has been disputed, especially by the later Buddhist philosophical school of thought, the Prasangika.[11]

MATTHYSSE: My question concerns the infinite chain of causes and effects in empirical phenomena. Western science has, of course, explored this and I think it could be said that as far as the ultimate metaphysical reference of the symbols in our physical science is concerned, we know very little. The more we advance into modern, physical ideas, the less we understand what these symbols mean. Bertrand Russell once said that it was like a genealogy, a pedigree, with no members in it; all structure and no substance. Nevertheless, there is an extraordinarily beautiful and precise mathematical structure. In other words, the flux, the succession of events, seems to be governed by mathematical principles that are extraordinarily precise and, in a sense, very beautiful, but these principles do not seem to have much to do with human needs and desires.

As I interpret your earlier talk, the invisible workings of karma are at the root of this flux and these have to do with motivation, the consequences of actions and so forth. But it is hard to understand how the flux could be regulated by two different principles at the same time. So my question is: What is the role and what is your understanding of the mathematical, elegant structure that seems to govern empirical phenomena?

DALAI LAMA: First, I think it would be useful to reflect on a fundamental metaphysical view in Buddhist philosophy, the doctrine of emptiness. In essence, this says that the fact that things exist is very obvious and apparent; our experience of interacting with physical reality and matter is sufficient evidence for us to accept this. The question is, in what manner do they exist?

Upon examining the ultimate nature of reality, Buddhist philosophers have concluded that things lack inherent existence, that is, they do not have self-defining, self-evident characteristics. This is because if we search for the essence of matter in whatever object it may be, we discover that it is unfindable, and when we subject things to ultimate analysis, we find that they do not exist as they appear to. Therefore, by subjecting the nature of reality to such analysis, we find that things do not have the solid, objective reality that they appear to have, that there is a discrepancy between the way things appear and the way in which they exist. This conclusion prevents us from falling into the extreme of absolutism, from holding on to some kind of absolutist view of reality. At the same time, because our empirical experience validates the existence of phenomena and is all the evidence we need that things exist, we cannot deny the nominal existence of things. This frees us from falling into the extreme of nihilism.

The question then arises, if things neither exist as they appear nor possess this objective reality, while at the same time they do exist, what then is their mode of existence? Buddhism explains that they exist only conventionally, in relative terms.

I wonder whether one can say that things exist mathematically[12] from the modern, scientific point of view? Is that possible?

MATTHYSSE: I think the first thing I would emphasize is that we have no idea what lies at the end of our symbols or equations, and there may be nothing lying at the end of our symbols and equations.

We would not say that things exist mathematically, because mathematical symbols do not actually refer to things at all. What then do they refer to? They seem to be conditions on our existence or our experience. They seem to describe it, so we can say that our experience has something about it that is very precise and very exact. That is all I would claim for mathematics, not that there are Platonic realities that inhere in matter, nothing like that.

DALAI LAMA: I would like to refer back to one of the points I raised before when talking about the invisible workings of karmic force. In the case of a flower, for example, the fact that it exists as a physical object and has come into existence through successive stages of its earlier moments cannot be described as the workings of karma. It is simply natural law that allows it to exist in this way.

MATTHYSSE: In other words, you do not think of everything that happens in the world as governed by the workings of karma?

DALAI LAMA: No. As I mentioned earlier, the space particle, the original source, eventually developed such that a certain part became a flower, a certain part became human flesh and so forth. When the existence of these two things causes particular experiences—pain, happiness and so on—it is then that the karmic link is involved. So it is only when the existence of external objects causes sentient beings to experience things like pain and pleasure that the karmic force comes into the picture.

For instance, the types of molecule and the molecular patterns required for this plant to exist in its particular form cannot be described as the workings of karma. Personally, I still find it quite difficult to determine exactly where the invisible workings of karma cease and the operation of natural laws begins. Even in the case of human experience, since we have certain physiological structures within our body, there are natural laws that govern our bodily experiences, but I myself am unclear as to the exact demarcation between these and other types of experience that are the products of our karmic force.

Karma means action, and this implies motivation. Any event, internal or external—anything that results from a sentient being's action driven by a motivating force—can be described as a product of karma. Our innate desire to enjoy happiness, for example, cannot be described as a product of karma because it is something natural to our existence. Similarly, the fact that cognitive events and mental states exist as mind and physical objects as matter, is simply the consequence of natural law and cannot be described as the product of karma.

SCHILDKRAUT: Can you tell us how the doctrine of emptiness applies to the ultimate nature of mind?

DALAI LAMA: Emptiness is the ultimate nature of reality in the sense that it is the mere absence of the inherent nature, or reified projection, that we impute on reality. The mind is also devoid of such reified existence and this aspect of mind is known as the emptiness of mind.

Emptiness plays a crucial role in Buddhist discussions and occupies an important place in Buddhist literature. This is because Buddhism maintains that at the root of our many psychological and emotional problems lies a fundamental misconception of reality. We have an innate belief in the existence of things as they appear to us and are ignorant of the discrepancy between the appearance of things and their true mode of existence. Because of this innate belief in the validity of appearances, we automatically grasp on to things as enduring entities that possess self-defining characteristics, essential natures, and this leads to all our confusion, psychological disturbances and so forth. Buddhism claims that it is only through understanding the true nature of reality by gaining insight into this essencelessness, the emptiness of things, that one can dispel all this psychological and emotional confusion. Gaining such insight definitely opens up the mind and makes an individual more flexible and open towards various possibilities.

Buddhist thinkers also find it extremely beneficial to incorporate into their thinking the insights of various scientific fields, such as quantum mechanics and neurobiology, where there are also equally strong elements of uncertainty and essencelessness.

SCHWARTZ: I notice that you move back and forth between the words human being and sentient being. What is a sentient being and what is the range of sentient beings within the universe?

DALAI LAMA: The Tibetan word for sentient being is *sem-chen*. This has a very definite meaning, it is 'a being with mind'. Nevertheless, the question of whether certain plants are sentient beings or not is a very difficult one to settle. I am not really sure what 'sentient being' means in English. One of my scientist friends, the neurobiologist Dr. Francisco Varela, once defined sentient beings as 'living beings that have the capacity to move from one place to another'.

SCHWARTZ: Are all animals sentient?

DALAI LAMA: Yes, definitely. Amoebas, for example, are sentient.

SCHWARTZ: You speak of the essential nature of human beings and sentient beings as compassionate, that this is somehow their essence though it may be tainted by experience. Yet if we look at human experience, there are no people on this globe who are not tainted by what we would call in the Judeo-Christian tradition 'original sin', a love of evil and torture. There is no culture on this earth—or very few—that can claim not to have sinned in this way.

DALAI LAMA: Although according to the traditions that accept a Creator God human beings have their negative aspects, still since they are essentially God's creation, must they not also have some positive nature?

SCHWARTZ: Yes, but it seems that in Buddhist philosophy there is an especially strong assertion that the ultimate base of human beings is pure and good and rich.

DALAI LAMA: Another way of explaining this is to remember that even though we find negativity to be a part of human nature, there is a way to eliminate sin through confession, devotion and similar practices. This indicates that our basic nature is pure.

SCHWARTZ: But if we observe the behavior of animals we see that they also torture and kill, and there are suggestions that some higher social beings within the animal realm indulge in behaviors similar to the uglier sides of human beings. So, if we look to nature as a guide to how things are, it would seem that evil and aggression are a very fundamental part of reality.

DALAI LAMA: My belief may be too simple, but I feel that from birth to death affection is the most important basis for the very existence of all sentient beings, particularly humans. Negative factors, such as anger and aggression, are a part of our human make-up, but I do not think that they are the main, dominant forces.

This is true even from the time of conception, during gestation and at the time of birth. Most obviously, on the day of birth, a baby will quite naturally accept milk from its mother or anyone else who feeds it with very sincere and genuine affection. And without this, the baby cannot possibly survive. Some medical scientists say that the first few weeks following birth are a crucial period for the growth of the brain and that the physical touch of the mother or someone else is vital for the healthy development of the baby's brain. So just as a flower needs the right temperature and moisture to grow properly, human beings need the warmth of affection for the parts of their physical body to develop correctly. Thus, the affection of others is a very positive factor in proper human development.

POTTER: I am a cellular scientist and a notorious radical materialist. I have a question that may be shared by other scientists or neuroscientists, as to whether one should invoke a non-material mind in order to understand brain science, or increase our understanding of human behavior.

You have talked about the way in which science works. Good scientists work very hard to make sure that there is an agreement about the facts, what behavior actually occurs, and then to interpret the facts. Of course, in natural science many interpretations are possible. Things are accepted as true in natural science not because they are the only explanation we can think of but because they are the explanation we prefer. My question concerns what explanation we prefer given the facts that are now commonly seen in neuroscience, and I will illustrate our dilemma with a particular case of behavior, the behavior of cocaine and particularly crack addicts.

Crack addicts display some behavior that is abnormal. It is the same kind of behavior seen in other drug abusers but exaggerated, and it is the biggest mental brain disorder presently afflicting this country. The clinical facts are these, and I will emphasize only a few of them. Crack addicts experience euphoria, and psychiatrists report that the euphoria is lifelong. There are two peculiar facts: a simple molecule produces euphoria, and causes lifelong memory of the euphoria. This euphoria is characterized as more intense than any other euphoric experience that the addict has experienced but not as an abnormal feeling created by a simple molecule. It is a curious and interesting feature that addicts report this feeling to be a perfectly familiar and normal one, but simply very exaggerated. So this is something that one must explain in brain science: How can a simple molecule produce this important emotion and so intensely?

Addicts show other behavior that needs an explanation. They become totally focused on using the drug and their use is out of control. A crack addict may smoke crack for several days. As long as the addict has crack he or she will continue to smoke it and do nothing else. They will not even eat food and consequently their health deteriorates. Drug abuse is defined as an out-of-control use of a drug. The picture is one of compelled behavior, and it would appear that ordinary mechanisms of will break down. Evidently, the action of this simple molecule is to produce in the addict a state in which no active consciousness and no active mind, coarse or clear, controls their behavior. Another fact is that this addiction remains throughout the person's life. In current practice we do not know how to cure it. The best we can hope for is to diminish the probability of relapse. A final effect is to cause people to be very sensitive to the environment in which the drug is used.

Now, how is this to be understood? In current brain science we see cocaine as acting on a well-defined group of nerve cells that secretes the substance dopamine at a particular place in the brain. The action of the simple cocaine molecule is to enhance the action of dopamine. It does this by combining with a particular membrane molecule that under normal circumstances takes up the dopamine and restricts its action. Crack-cocaine prevents this uptake. What cocaine seems to be doing in this cellular system is prolonging the action of the brain mechanism whose normal role is to tell the rest of the brain, whatever you just did, do it again, and put the circumstances into memory so that you can come back here and do it again. Of course, in the evolution of sentient beings such a mechanism would have been very important, provided it was controlled in a normal way. In people like us, there are shreds of evidence that when this system is activated the conscious experience is euphoria. The evidence is not very strong, the number of people who have been investigated is very small, but there is strong reason to believe that cocaine activates the system that leads to this emotion, euphoria, and that, of course, is a strong reason for people to take this drug under circumstances where their life is not euphoric.

Current neuroscientists are working very hard and taxpayers' money is being spent in large amounts to investigate this system. The assumption is that we will understand euphoria and compelled behavior in terms of cellular neuroscience, or neuroscience in general. There is very little motivation under such circumstances to assume that what crack is really doing is acting on a non-material, clear and formless mind. We think that it is working on nerve cells, and our judgment about the way to proceed is to continue on this line.

Now, this kind of observation makes neuroscientists increasingly less interested in seeking explanations for why we do what we do in terms of a non-material, clear and formless mind. (I should add that the particular nerve cells upon which cocaine is known to act are neither clear nor formless; they are amazingly intricate in shape and they occur in collections of nerve cells whose form is wonderfully intricate. They are not clear, they contain a pigment, and that is unusual in the brain, though no one knows whether it is related in any way to these phenomena.)

So there is wide agreement on the facts that I have just described. Everyone assumes that anyone who tries these experiments will reach the same conclusion. However, the implication of these facts is very uncomfortable in Western philosophy and theology. I do not know of any scientist who feels comfortable with them. They come as a surprise and are not something that we can intuit from our own experience.

There is a tendency, when we deal with bad behavior, to assume that it is done by nerve cells and to be comfortable with this fact, but not to feel like this about normal behavior. Of course this is foolish. It is not likely that nature endowed us with this amazingly intricate system of nerve cells simply so that they can go awry and give us unwholesome behavior like drug abuse. We have to assume that normal behavior is also controlled by these cells. They have a normal role.

Because of these observations, many of which are present in everyday life, one is led to wonder whether decisions are ever made in consciousness or whether the consciousness in which we take so much pride is simply a reporter function in the brain. Are decisions and emotions calculated by nerve cells whose behavior we cannot bring into consciousness and cannot control by conscious mechanisms? This is very uncomfortable in Western science. Is it all right in Buddhist science?

DALAI LAMA: As I mentioned earlier, Buddhists would also agree to a certain extent on the importance of understanding the physiological states of the body. One cannot understand visual perception, for example, in isolation from the sense organ of the eye. Similarly, there are various mental states that cannot be understood in isolation from the physiological state of the brain. So the effects of drugs that you see in the brains of addicts are, from the Buddhist point of view, effects at a gross level of mind.

In tantric literature we find descriptions of various meditative techniques aimed primarily at controlling a person's physiological states by applying such techniques as yoga, concentration on energy channels and so forth. These meditations are intended to neutralize the meditator's physiological forces so that they cannot influence his or her fundamental clear light mind. I feel that there is some parallel here with what you said about the effects of cocaine.

But I would like to ask you a question: Have you done any experiments on two different subjects, where one is very strong-willed and the other very weak-willed? Is there any difference in effect when the same dose of drug is given to a weak-willed person and to a strongly-resistant person who knows how negative drugs are?

POTTER: There has never been a good controlled experiment with human beings, but the common experience of clinicians who treat addicts is that people who are depressed, anxious and under stress are especially vulnerable. However, we all share this brain mechanism and clinicians are clear that every one of us is vulnerable. Every one of us can become an addict, and especially when under stress.

DALAI LAMA: But is there a difference between these two people? One is weak-willed and the other strong-willed, and while they may experience similar physiological states, hallucinations, euphoria and so forth, would the first not be more likely to take drugs again than the second, who is convinced that taking drugs is very destructive?

Or, in the case of alcoholism, is there any difference between two alcoholics, one who makes a very strong decision in the morning that he is not going to get drunk that day and later has a drink, and another who never makes that kind of strong determination but drinks an equal amount of alcohol?

Most of us have had the experience of going to bed with the determination of awaking at a particular time. What difference would you see between that and going to bed without such a determination? The sleep is the same, yet would you find a difference?

POTTER: We are widely different types of people. We are not identical except for the identical twins amongst us, and even amongst identical twins there are differences in behavior. The concordance of alcoholism among identical twins in families where alcoholism has been a big problem is only about seventy per cent. So yes, people can differ in their response to the drugs. The message seems to be that we have a system that makes us all vulnerable and the extent of our vulnerability depends on the details of our circumstances. No doubt many abusers would be very much helped by your methods.

BEAR: I think we have a very clear example of how differently human beings respond to the presence of certain drugs. We have probably all received some kind of a strong pain reliever, often of the opiate class and potentially an addicting drug, when in hospital. Yet virtually none of the people given these drugs, who are on the whole, happy, adjusted people in need of a medical procedure, develop an addiction. Unhappy people, however, whether the unhappiness comes from a bad family, poverty or other factors, are very prone to addiction, and in seeking the drug may then injure others, steal and perform bad acts. So there is objective evidence that people are quite different; something about the environment changes even what seems to be a physiological reaction.

Let me now turn that into a general question. Most of us, as scientists or doctors who think about mind, start with some presumptions: that the human nervous system, or brain, is the place where many operations relevant to mind occur; that neurons and nerve cells are the operating principles; and that chemicals may send the signals. In the Western tradition, we also tend to believe in evolution: that simpler organisms existed first; that through some random events and selection, more and more complex groups of nerve cells developed; and that eventually a larger and more complex brain, the human brain, developed from these simpler brains. We think we have evidence that within our very large brain particular parts of it perform different jobs. One area is involved with visual signals, for example, and even in the parts that deal with emotions, we think that certain structures—the amygdala—are very important for feeling certain states.

For example, there is a rather easy way to understand some forms of aggression in the human brain from the viewpoint of evolution. If we evolved from simple creatures, they had to be aggressive. They had to protect their offspring, they had to fight to protect territory and at times to win food. And we have inherited some of the same nerve structures. We have also inherited other structures that turn off aggression. Even compassion, in this evolutionary model, may come out of other behaviors. If a creature is kind to its close relatives, the genes that we think carry this information will stay around in the gene pool. Thus altruism and compassion might be explained as coming out of evolution.

It seems to me that the Buddhist approach is rather different. It does not start with this idea of evolution from the simple but assumes that mind is present from the very beginning. Can you find any common ground between these two points of view?

DALAI LAMA: I feel that these two are compatible. When I mentioned that Buddhism assumes that mind exists from the beginning, I was referring to the fundamental existence of mind, which is in the pure nature of knowing and clarity, and which is formless. But when we discuss the various forms of cognitive and mental events, it becomes more complex. These events have to be explained in relation to the physiological basis on which they arise, and the different forms and states of cognitive and mental events are also very much dependent upon the external environment.

So when we talk about mind in the Buddhist context, you should not have the notion that it is a single, substantial entity but rather a very complex network of interrelated cognitive and mental events. One could even assert that there are as many mental events as there are external matters. In other words, the multitude of mental and cognitive events corresponds to an equal multitude of external objects that serve as their causal condition and to the physiological bases such as the sense organs.

Now, I would like to ask a question. It has been several years since the advent of neuroscience. During this same period, our rapidly advancing technology has led to a new way of life being developed, the use of computers and so forth demanding increased speed in thought, calculation and so on. Have neuroscientists observed any physiological changes in the human brain as a result of the computer revolution? Can you see the possibility of changes in human brain structure, not necessarily immediately but, say, over the next hundred years?

BEAR: We believe that the human brain is changing rather slowly and, in fact, the human brain is already so complex that it is probably teaching us better ways to build computers. One area of study is called the 'neuronet model'. This is based on trying to make computers do some of what our brains have probably been doing for thousands of years. So we believe that evolutionary change is taking place, but, in terms of computer science, we probably have not learned one tenth of what is going on in our mind.

I would like to ask whether some of the mental practices of 'emptying the self' could be compatible with the idea that our brain has been built over millions of years of evolution. Can we ever turn away from our biological past?

DALAI LAMA: In the Buddhist description of mind and mental events there is no assumption that every cognitive event has to be conscious; unconscious levels of mind are also described. There is an assumption in the West that when Buddhism describes the existence of consciousness, or mind, it is referring to a substantial entity independent of the body, but this is a misunderstanding. In Buddhism, mind cannot be understood in isolation from the body. It is a very complex network of interrelated mental events.

The reason why Buddhists do not accept the existence of an independent I, self, or eternal soul abiding within the body is because they conceive mind not so much as a substantial entity independent of the body but rather as a dynamic, ever-present process very intimately connected to and related with the physiological states of the body. Therefore, to postulate an independent, eternal soul does not fit with basic Buddhist philosophy. The crucial point is, what is it that can eventually be separated from the body of the human being?—It is the subtlest level of mind, the clear light mind. But we can experiment on that mind only when the person is clinically dead!

Now, among meditators we find a very unusual phenomenon. A person may be pronounced clinically dead—that is, the brain no longer functions and there is no respiration—but the body does not decompose for one, two, or in some cases several weeks. We say that the meditator is in the clear light state.

This phenomenon occurs quite naturally at the time of death, but if a meditator who has acquired certain meditative skills can simulate the death experience while still alive, then it is claimed that he or she can consciously separate the mind from the body and have an out-of-body experience. Once that state of mind has been reached through meditation, all the gross levels of mind that depend heavily on the physical body dissolve and cease, and at that moment the person can, theoretically, separate mind from body intentionally.

BENSON: His Holiness and I have been talking for ten years now about the possibility of measuring people in the clear light state—that is, after they have passed away—to find out what is going on. But we have had a logistic problem with travelling between Boston and Dharamsala in enough time to work this out!

BEAR: Is it then taught that some aspects of the mind are independent of the brain cells or the body?

DALAI LAMA: Ultimately I do not know. The most subtle level of consciousness can be separate from the body, but we cannot call that subtlest level of mind the *human* mind because 'human mind' is a relative term used only in relation to a human body.

BENSON: One problem that Western science has been struggling with for over a hundred years is how much of our daily existence is dictated by what we inherit, our genetics, and how much can be influenced by our minds. It used to be thought that genetics were more important than environment. Then there was a time when we said that environment was more important than genetics. Now the genetic argument is coming back. What does Tibetan Buddhism say to this? How much of our lives is dictated by what we inherit and how much can we truly influence?

DALAI LAMA: Just as the influence of genetic inheritance is very powerful, so too is the influence of the environment on the mind. These concepts seem to be in accord with the Buddhist approach. For instance, when we read the guidelines for meditators, we find strong emphasis being placed on their seeking solitary places for their practice, at least in the initial stages. This is because the environment has a very powerful effect on a person's mental state. We also find descriptions in Buddhist literature of how various emotional states such as anger, hatred, jealousy and desire can be dominant in some people's minds and less dominant in others', and this shows that there is a strong element of inheritance involved.

POTTER: Your Holiness, as a measure of the self-confidence and high morale of both brain scientists and people who work on artificial intelligence, that is to say, computer mimics of human intelligence, I would like to ask you one final question. If, at some future time when our ignorance is not so great, you could make by genetic engineering, with proteins and amino acids, or by engineering with chips and copper wires, an organism that had all of our good qualities and none of our bad ones, would you do it? Would this not be an interesting form of incarnation?

DALAI LAMA: If this were possible it would be most welcome. It would save a lot of effort!

3

Mind/Body Interaction including Tibetan Studies

Herbert Benson, MD
Associate Professor of Medicine, Harvard Medical School;
President, Mind/Body Medical Institute

Mind/Body Interactions including Tibetan Studies

My topic is mind/body interactions. I will emphasize some of the studies we have had the honor of performing with the Tibetan Buddhist community over this last decade. To place this in proper perspective, I will briefly review our earliest findings with respect to meditation. I will also define the relaxation response and how research into this evolved into our work with His Holiness the Dalai Lama and the Tibetan Buddhist community.

Our work dates back more than twenty years, when we became interested in how high blood pressure might be influenced by emotions. To that end, I returned to the physiological laboratories at the Harvard Medical School, of which Dr. A. Clifford Barger was chief. There, while experiments were being performed, some young people came to me and essentially said, 'Why don't you study us? We think we can effectively control our blood pressure; we practice transcendental meditation.' Now this was 1967 and it was Harvard Medical School, so with some hesitation I started a series of experiments on people who practice transcendental meditation. (I would like to point out at this juncture that there is nothing unique about transcendental meditation; it was simply the first model in which we studied the physiological changes that occur during the meditational process.) Collaborators in this work were Dr. Robert Keith Wallace and Dr. Archie F. Wilson of the University of California at Irvine.

We brought healthy meditators to the laboratory and instrumented them with intravenous catheters, intra-arterial catheters, electrodes to measure their heart rate and rhythm, electrodes to measure their brainwaves and masks to capture their expired breath so that we could measure their metabolism. Then, we had them sit for an entire hour before the measurements began.

The experiment was divided into three periods. There was a pre-meditational period, a meditational period and a post-meditational period, each lasting twenty minutes. After the initial measurements were taken during the first twenty minutes of the pre-meditational period, the subjects were asked to meditate. If you looked at them you saw no change in their activity, no change in their posture—they simply changed the content of their thought. They used their mind differently. While they did so we continued to measure the physiological changes for the next twenty minutes during the meditational period. At the end of that time, we asked them to go back to their regular mode of thinking. Again they changed their way of thinking. There were dramatic changes in oxygen consumption, which is the medical term for metabolism. In other words, their overall metabolism, their overall energy consumption decreased 16 and 17 per cent with the simple process of changing their thinking. (Please keep these percentages in mind because, as we will see later, more profound changes were found in more advanced meditators in some of our studies with Tibetan Buddhists.)

Paralleling the changes in oxygen consumption were changes in the elimination of carbon dioxide, which is the waste product of metabolism. These subjects were truly decreasing their metabolism—they were burning less body fuel by thinking differently, by meditating.

Their rate of breathing also decreased from about 13 to 14 breaths per minute to 10 or 11 breaths per minute, by simply changing their thinking. This was not a conscious action to breathe slower. It was simply that the respiration decreased because they required less oxygen. Furthermore, after an initial decrease, there was a significant decrease in minute ventilation, the amount of air moving in and out of the lungs. There was no change in the PO_2—that is, the concentration of oxygen in the arterial blood. The cells were getting enough fuel, oxygen; they were simply using less. There was also a precipitous fall in the arterial blood lactate. High levels of lactate are associated with anxiety, disquietude; low levels with peace and tranquility. Here, we found some of the lowest levels ever recorded in man. There was no change in rectal temperature, which essentially told us that this was not a state of hibernation.

Then we asked the question, could it be sleep? With the practice of meditation, decreases in oxygen consumption (metabolism) occurred within three to five minutes and lasted as long as the meditation continued. There was a return to normal metabolism when regular thoughts returned. In contrast, during sleep there is a slow, progressive decrease from one to two to three to four to five to six hours. Furthermore, the brainwave changes were somewhat different from those of sleep.

We believe that what was occurring during meditation was a response that is opposite to the stress response. During the stress response, the so-called 'fight-or-flight' response, there are increases in metabolism, blood pressure, heart rate and respiration rate.

Over the years, we found that two basic steps are necessary to bring forth this response during meditation, a response we have labelled the 'relaxation response'. The relaxation response is not unique to transcendental meditation, but is shared by any process incorporating the two basic steps that bring about these physiological changes: (1) the repetition of a word, sound, prayer, thought, phrase or even a muscular activity, and (2) disregard of other thoughts that come to mind and passive return to the repetition.

These instructions are embedded in religious and secular techniques that have existed for thousands and thousands of years. We found that the only difference between them in eliciting the relaxation response was in the choice of the word, sound or prayer. One finds different words chosen in the Hindu tradition, for example, than in the Jewish tradition; the instructions are the same but the words are different. Within Christianity, certain prayers dating back to the time of Christ himself have evolved that involve the same steps. These prayers are now within Catholicism and various forms of Protestantism. Within Tibetan Buddhism, a common phrase is OM MANI PADME HUM, repeated over and over. The point is that the relaxation response is a common human physiologic response and a part of all religions that utilize repetitious prayer.

When this response is elicited repeatedly, it can counteract the harmful effects of stress. Over the past twenty years, this usefulness has been demonstrated by our laboratory and others in the treatment of any disorder that is related to the opposite response, the stress response. So the relaxation response is now working its way into modern medicine. It is a recommended therapy for hypertension, cardiac arrhythmias, chronic pain and insomnia; for the side effects of cancer therapy and AIDS therapy; for the psychological conditions of anxiety, hostility and depression; for premenstrual tension and infertility; and as preparation for X-ray and surgical procedures. At the

New England Deaconess Hospital and other hospitals throughout this country and the world, these techniques are being applied to interact with the awesome treatments of modern medicine. The two can be combined rather well.

However, a question remained: If a simple mental technique could bring forth such profound and healthy physiologic changes, how far could the mind go to bring about other physiologic changes? In this context, I had the honor to first meet His Holiness the Dalai Lama in 1979 at Harvard. On that occasion, I explained what I have just discussed and asked whether it would be possible to study advanced Tibetan Buddhist meditational practices, such as *gTum-mo* yoga.

gTum-mo yoga is a practice that I first learned of through the writings of the late Alexandra David-Neel.[13] Disguised as a Tibetan monk at the turn of the century, she travelled throughout Tibet and later published her observations. One of the things she observed was seeing monks in midwinter performing a type of meditation called *gTum-mo* yoga, which, of course, is a religious rite. The monks were testing their proficiency at this meditation, which is performed to generate an internal body heat that will burn away the defilements of improper thinking, and they were observed to melt the snow around them where they sat. In fact, their proficiency at *gTum-mo* was measured by the extent to which the snow was melted. They were also observed drying icy wet sheets on their bodies in midwinter by generating this heat.

I asked His Holiness whether it would be possible to study such people. He agreed, and this has led to a number of expeditions to India to study *gTum-mo* and other meditative phenomena.

To understand *gTum-mo*, or the effects of *gTum-mo*, I would like to put it into the context of our Western understanding of temperature regulation. When an animal or a human is placed in a cool or cold environment, there are two ways in which heat can be maintained within the body in order to stay alive: heat conservation and heat production.

Let us look first at heat production. There are different ways in which warm-blooded animals can produce heat. There can be chemical stimulation, through epinephrine, thyroxin and other chemicals. Epinephrine and thyroxin are hormones that increase metabolism and generate heat. Animals can also generate heat through increased muscular activity. In fact, the muscles have been called the 'furnaces' of the body. Increasing the tone of the muscles through shivering, for example, generates more heat. We can also generate heat voluntarily by moving about or exercising. When people are cold they often jump up and down or move their arms back and forth to warm up.

Now let us look at heat conservation. When we are placed in a cool or cold environment, there are two ways in which we can conserve heat: through non-circulatory and circulatory factors. First, non-circulatory factors: To decrease heat loss we can decrease the amount of our body surface exposed to the air by hunkering down, so that we act less as radiators. Another method is piloerection. This is not so relevant for humans, but animals can raise their hair up to create an extra layer of insulation. Animals can also increase the weight of their fur and, in conditions of long-term exposure to the cold, store more fat under the skin. As humans, we simply put on extra clothing to conserve heat.

The circulatory factors that decrease heat loss are as follows: One thing we do is to cool the blood that is going to our extremities. Our fingers get cold, for example, because we shut down the amount of blood flowing to our fingers to prevent it from being cooled. In fact, the reason why our fingers and toes get cold when we are moved into cool or cold environments is because, if you want to argue teleologically, we try to conserve heat in the places where it is really needed—the heart, lungs and brain. In a cool or cold environment, the blood vessels clamp down so that less blood is exposed to the skin and less heat is lost. There are specific areas of the body that exhibit this cooling more than others, and some parts of the body may get so cold that frost-bite occurs, that is, the tissue actually dies. This occurs most often in the fingers, toes and ears—exposed parts of our body that have a lot of surface area—and to a lesser extent in the heel of the foot, the nose, the face and other areas.

So when we are placed in a cool or cold environment, our fingers and toes and other areas of the skin get cooler; that is a normal response. Now what was happening in *gTum-mo*, or what was allegedly happening in *gTum-mo*, was just the opposite. The monks practicing *gTum-mo* were allegedly able to generate increases in their skin temperature when it should have been decreasing.

We travelled to northern India to perform research on *gTum-mo*.

The first monk we studied lived on a ridge high in the mountains above Dharamsala. The air temperature there was about 16 °C (roughly 60 °F), which is a cool to cold environment. We would perceive that as being quite cool if we were undressed and naked, and we would have cooler fingers and toes. Despite the cool/cold environment, as the *gTum-mo* progressed, the monk's finger and toe temperatures increased markedly.

We then studied a second monk and found the same phenomenon.[14] In this monk, while in a 20 °C environment, which is also perceived to be cool to cold, there was a marked increase in finger and toe temperature during the practice of *gTum-mo*. In this case, when the *gTum-mo* stopped, the finger temperature also decreased. A third monk was studied in a 16 °C environment and again increased skin temperature was noted.

What was happening here was in direct opposition to what one would have predicted. A cooling and decrease in the temperature of fingers and toes should have occurred, but actually, during the practice of *gTum-mo*, the skin temperature of the fingers and toes increased.

On another expedition, we sent a film team to Manali. There we were able to study monks who had spent an entire year practicing *gTum-mo*. On a night considered to be the coldest of the year, the first full moon of that period, and in a room temperature of 40 °F, just a few degrees above freezing, these monks dipped sheets into icy water and then taking these dripping wet sheets, which measured some 3 x 6 feet, wrapped their essentially naked bodies in them. You and I would shiver uncontrollably and perhaps even die if we did this, but here, within three to five minutes the sheets started to steam and within forty-five minutes were completely dry. The monks repeated this process twice more before dawn. It was truly remarkable.

We then tried to measure oxygen consumption during the practice of *gTum-mo* to see if an increased amount of energy was being generated by *gTum-mo* that would account for the heat. So the next step was to return with the proper equipment to take measurements of metabolism. This was done in 1988, when we travelled to Rumtek Monastery in Sikkim, which is at an altitude of about 7,000 feet.

Three monks were studied. Two of the monks increased their overall oxygen consumption during *gTum-mo* and after *gTum-mo*. To our complete surprise, the third monk exhibited not an increase in metabolism, but a striking decrease in metabolism. If you will remember, earlier we had found a 16 to 17 per cent decrease in oxygen consumption during simple meditation. This third monk, during his resting meditation, decreased his oxygen consumption an astounding 64 per cent. This is the largest decrease in metabolism ever recorded from rest. His respiratory rate decreased from a normal of fourteen breaths per minute to five or six breaths per minute. (I think this perhaps explains how Indian yogis can be buried alive for long periods of time. They decrease their energy metabolism to such an extent that they can extract enough oxygen from the soil to stay alive for prolonged periods.) I later discussed some of these experiments with His Holiness. Without knowing the data, His Holiness said of these three monks that one was thought not to be very good at *gTum-mo*. Those who made this assessment were correct, however the monk is obviously very good at something else!

What we are finding through these experiments is that meditative processes lead to rather striking physiological changes in the body. These changes have direct health implications to the extent that any disorder is caused or made worse by stress. These very simple processes are quite appropriate in the treatment of stress-related disorders, and they are in no way incompatible with modern medicine; the two can work side by side as they do at the New England Deaconess Hospital.

We are dedicated to understanding how the mind can influence the body. To this end, we will continue our relationship with the Tibetan Buddhists to see how much we can learn from each other, and we will pass on this knowledge so that people can learn to help themselves in a responsible fashion that is based upon scientific study.

Questions from the Audience

QUESTION: One similar condition that you did not mention is that of hypnosis. Have you studied this in terms of metabolism?

BENSON: Yes. Hypnosis is a trance-like state. There are two phases to hypnosis. The first phase of hypnosis is the pre-suggestion phase. The physiology of this phase is indistinguishable from that of meditation and the relaxation response. Then hypnosis goes into the suggestion phase: A suggestion is made and the physiological changes are consistent with those suggested. So there is an initial commonality between hypnosis and the relaxation response, but then hypnosis goes its own direction.

QUESTION: I have breast cancer that has spread to both of my lungs and I would like to know how I can heal my cancer and come to terms with dying.

BENSON: I am certain your concern is shared with many others. At the Deaconess Hospital, we have groups that deal with cancer on the basis of the relaxation response. What we and others[15] are finding is that processes that elicit the relaxation response seem to prolong the lifetime of those who are suffering from cancer. Furthermore, we are finding within our groups that many of the psychological and physiological changes that accompany the anxiety and depression about the cancer can be reversed; people have less depression, less anxiety and less hostility as they complete our groups. We are continuing to utilize these scientifically-based mind/body processes in the treatment of cancer. One notable finding is that the nausea and vomiting caused by chemotherapy are markedly decreased by the use of these techniques.

QUESTION: The religious traditions that you described as having evoked, or seemed to evoke, the relaxation response appear to be traditions of one-pointed meditation, of focusing repeatedly on coming back again and again to a phrase or an image. Have you done any studies on different kinds of meditation, particularly mindfulness meditation, where the aim might not be to return again and again to a single point but to be aware of whatever comes up?

BENSON: It has been shown both in our work and in the work of others that there is a common physiological state, a doorway that one passes through, with the simple forms of meditation. Once through that doorway, one emerges with, if you will, a more quiet, receptive mind, and other thought processes can then take the physiology in different directions.

What is occurring in Western medicine now is that we are investigating how one can use one's thoughts after the doorway is opened. For example, in the treatment of cancer, techniques now being used include visualizing the white cells of the body attacking the cancer cells. At least now there is a formula, a path that can be followed. Through continued study of Tibetan Buddhism and other cultures, but particularly Tibetan Buddhism because of their extensive expertise, we hope to study further mind/body changes. I believe this speaks directly to what His Holiness discussed earlier about the capabilities of mind to effect yet other physiological changes.

QUESTION: Your studies emphasize oxygen a great deal. Did any of these studies measure either carbon dioxide or PCO_2 levels and/or pH levels in the blood? And if so, what did you find?

BENSON: There is a slight metabolic acidosis that occurs during the practice of the relaxation response—metabolic acidosis as opposed to a respiratory acidosis. We do not fully understand this. We measured the carbon dioxide in the expired air and it paralleled the changes in the oxygen. In other words, the respiratory quotient remained unchanged.

QUESTION: Was metabolic acidosis defined as a major pH change as well as a lactate?

BENSON: No, it was a minor change. But the metabolic acidosis is opposite to what would be predicted by the lactate changes. We do not understand this.

QUESTION: Could you speculate a little, after doing ten-plus years of this kind of research, what some of its potentials could be? You have certainly shown that you can influence some physiological changes. I wonder if there are any theories that you are working toward and what potential you can see?

BENSON: We cannot predict where this work will take us. It is relatively new to Western science. That is why it is so important that we have the privilege to interact with another culture that has been dedicated to the understanding of how these mind states can be utilized. How far this can go, I am not sure, but I think it would be a terrible mistake to think that what we are doing is in any way counter to modern medicine. A challenge is to appropriately combine what others can do for us and what we can do for ourselves.

QUESTION: Is a higher altitude better for meditation?

BENSON: I know of no evidence that meditation is more effective at different altitudes.

QUESTION: At what age can a child meditate effectively?

BENSON: Various traditions have shown that very young children can learn these processes, but they are made simpler and phrased differently. For example, a child might be asked to repeat a short phrase as he or she walks around in a circle. Here again, we can learn from other cultures where this is developed. In the Hindu culture, for example, children can learn to carry out these practices at the age of four or five.

QUESTION: Can you explain how the distractions of the instruments, the mask, the hose and so on did not interfere with the successful practice of meditation?

BENSON: More than the hoses, I have often wondered about the rectal thermometers. People are able to focus through distractions. It is just the way one deals with extraneous thoughts by centering back upon a meditative focus. One can essentially disregard the thought that there is a mask by keeping the mind on the focus of meditation. It can be done, as these experiments testify.

QUESTION: His Holiness explained to us that there is a more subtle aspect of the mind—and possibly many such aspects—not bound by the body. Many people will have experienced some of these aspects of the mind and be particularly interested in the possibilities of their external measurement or verification. Do you know what kind of progress has been made in this realm, and do you have any thoughts about it?

BENSON: I think that this symposium speaks to the attempts we are making to understand and measure, if you will, the more subtle aspects of mind. Indeed, this is the challenge for the future.

PART TWO

BUDDHISM, PSYCHOLOGY &
THE COGNITIVE SCIENCES

4

Tibetan Psychology: Sophisticated Software for the Human Brain

Robert A. F. Thurman, Ph.D

*Jey Tsong Khapa Professor of Indo-Tibetan Buddhist Studies,
Columbia University*

4

Tibetan Psychology: Sophisticated Software for the Human Brain

Psychology is the science of the mind. It is the 'inner science',[16] as they call it in India and Tibet, *par excellence*. In the West, it is the descendant of philosophy, natural philosophy, of both metaphysics—the quest of reality—and epistemology—the quest of valid knowledge. In India, science and philosophy have never split, philosophy always having been thought essential to control the theoretical part of science and ultimately to be indivisible from the empirical part. And within philosophy's sciences, the inner science, philosophy/psychology, has always been considered the king of all the sciences.

In India, the quest for the knowledge of reality has always been considered the eminently practical matter. As the great eighth-century Indian philosopher Dharmakirti said,[17] 'All successful human action proceeds from valid knowledge'. If humanity wants to succeed in any sense, it must gain valid knowledge of reality—the reality of self and the reality of the environment. We might add a corollary: All unsuccessful human action—and there seems to be quite a bit these days—proceeds from misknowledge, or ignorance. There could therefore be no higher priority in the life of the individual, or in the life of nations, than to conquer misknowledge and to gain valid knowledge.

In the West, scientists have predominantly thought of reality as external to the human thought world, as the physical world, the outer world, the world 'out there'. It has seemed to scientists that the environment needed to be tamed, controlled and engineered to suit human needs. Thus physics, chemistry, biology and astronomy, armed with mathematics and geometry, have been considered the most important sciences in the West. The psyche was left to the priests, who eventually differentiated into philosophers, poets, artists and psychiatrists. When psychology sought entry into the halls of science, rather recently, it tried to model itself on the 'hard' sciences.

Freud discovered for psychology an invisible realm of energies analogous to the macro realms of astronomers, the micro realms of biologists and chemists and the near mythical, subatomic realms of physicists. He then developed theories of the workings of the psyche's invisible, unconscious energies and the mechanism for observation of these workings through dreams. Jung expanded that mechanism to include the examination of the working of culture as dreams collectivized in myths, with formal elements analyzed into archetypes. Other psychologists eventually considered this approach too soft and so developed behaviorism to reduce the workings of the psyche to the observed behavior of body and speech.

Still today, the most powerful movement in psychology, or in the cognitive sciences, is neuroscience, which continues to reduce mind to physical processes in the brain, and to combine chemical, biological and biophysical approaches to understand and control that physical psyche, the brain/mind. The map of the cognitive sciences drawn by Howard Gardner in *The Mind's New Science*,[18] shows neuroscience as one of the six cognitive sciences, the others being philosophy, psychology, anthropology, artificial intelligence and linguistics. By far the most energy goes into neuroscience in terms of funds and preoccupation. Many experimental results have already been achieved and many more are to be reasonably expected. His Holiness and other Tibetan psychologists are fascinated by neuroscience and think of neuroscientists as promising participants in East/West dialogue.

I have set myself to address two main questions: First, why does modern, Western, cognitive science need the old-fashioned mind science of Tibet? And second, if the Indo-Tibetan tradition does have something to contribute, what is it? In what form would its contribution be made? And how could Western cognitive sciences best take advantage of it? Exploring the first requires realizing that Western science is dominated by materialism and then taking a critical look at scientific materialism's prospects for success in understanding the mind reduced to brain processes. Exploring the second requires giving a brief overview and some examples of Indo-Tibetan psychology. I will conclude with some practical recommendations.

In ancient India, when the Buddha established the Buddhist educational institutions, reality was approached as both outer environment and inner self, the same as in the West. The inner self, however, was chosen as the more important to understand and the more practical to control and engineer to suit human needs. This was not because of a naive belief in the irreducible human spirit or because of any sort of mysticism. Materialists were already flourishing at that time. The Buddhists themselves used materialistic reductionism in contexts where practical, especially in the development of medicine, the 'outer' science to which they gave the third greatest priority (after linguistics and logic).[19] Buddhists critically rejected the soul theories current in most religions of the time and did not consider any aspect of nature, inner or outer, mystically sacrosanct, beyond analysis and under-standing. Most important, the Buddhists made claim that their turn to inner science, mind science, as a top priority among the sciences, was based on a thorough and comprehensive knowledge of reality, on an already assessed, depth understanding of self and environment; that is to say, on the complete enlightenment of the Buddha. This was their claim, supported by the at-least partial enlightenments of his numerous colleagues and successors.

Naturally, this is a claim that we must treat today with a firm skepticism. We must doubt it. The Buddha himself would have wanted us to doubt his claim that he had become enlightened. He said, 'Doubt it, don't just accept it.' But we must doubt it in such a way that we examine whatever evidence is advanced, pro and con. We cannot afford to simply *dismiss* the claim *a priori* as if we, all unknow-ing as we profess to be, actually have at least the certainty that no one else ever did achieve certainty. We must consider the claim critically, and we must acknowledge that if it were possible for a human being to become all-knowing, even to the slightest degree, by a process of inner development, without external, mechanical aids, that it would be extremely significant. The examination and evaluation of such a process of inner development would become an important *scientific* task; not a religious quest, but a scientific task.

Underlying the choice of what aspect of reality, outer or inner, is more important to understand and control, is the complex of views about what reality is, what life within that reality is, what human life in particular is, what its purpose is and what its needs and prospects are. Without knowing the answers to these questions, if we just rush off and analyze aspects of the environment, modify what seems modifiable, and satisfy immediate needs without a long-term perspec-tive, our procedure is not likely to succeed. In fact, it is a procedure that has already brought us to a very dubious and dangerous situation.

Our present situation is that we have cumulatively developed an excellent knowledge of many aspects of our environment, without achieving a comprehensive knowledge of all its dimensions. Yet based on this partial knowledge, we have intervened deeply in the processes of nature. We have abolished many diseases and improved some conditions of life, to be sure, but thereby we have drastically unbalanced our population in relation to the Earth and our environment. We have created powerful machines that can do extraordinary things, but thereby we have depleted our resources and have polluted and strained to the danger point the natural balance. We have brought warfare to an unimaginable pitch of destructive efficiency, but thereby we have put ourselves in immediate danger of self-caused planetary extinction. In essence, our powers to affect the outer reality have far outstripped our powers over ourselves. This is the key point.

We are little more directly aware of our basic reality than any human beings have ever been. Most of our actions are based on penetrating and pervasive misknowledge of what we are doing, dressed up with hunches and guesses and degrees and certificates and mutual reassurances. Most of the time we are helplessly swayed by basic emotions of lust, greed, pride, envy and hatred. We quickly lose our self-control and commit actions that harm others and even ourselves in the long and sometimes short run. If such potentially angry and greedy people as we can be, were, on a fragile planet, to invent nuclear, chemical and biological weapons of immense mass destruction, put them into the hands of equally *un*self-controlled leaders who were then to unleash the unimaginable horrors of the technically-very-possible World War III, which was then to make all life on this planet impossible for hundreds of thousands of years . . . were that scenario to take place, then, whoever might be left to observe it would rightly say that the Greco-Roman, Euro-American decision to mess around with the environment without understanding and controlling the self was a fatally flawed, foolish and monstrous decision made by human beings who tragically thought that as Westerners, they were greatest, the smartest on the planet.

Personally I do not think this doomsday scenario will happen because I think that there is real intelligence in this universe, and we are more complex. As a civilization we have also been making efforts to understand and control ourselves. Though our Western efforts in this direction have rarely been *scientific* efforts, our religions and humanities have not been totally idle. I think we will make it. The point of rehearsing this scenario, however, is to appreciate how the Buddha and company might have foreseen the dangerous crisis humans could get into if they did not make self-understanding a higher priority than environmental domination. Therefore, I propose to you the radical idea that the Indian decision not to develop outer sciences, technology, the industrial machine—the whole thing we think of as Western civilization—might not simply be the result of a failure of intellect, but instead represent a great success of intellect. The failure of intellect might well be ours, expressed in our decision to interfere and tamper with everything, and so unleash physical powers without having any mental power. There is an important difference between just failing to do something and deciding not to do it. How well we understand this can very much affect the way we approach the science of another culture; whether from the paternalistic stance of our assumed superiority because we have the power to blow up the planet, or from an open-minded stance of humility because we might have made a wrong turn because we are about to blow up the planet. As you can see, these attitudes are very different. We must achieve humility here, if we are to benefit from the Indo-Tibetan development of *inner* science and inner technologies.

Western neuroscience approaches the human mind as a brain, a sophisticated, 'wetware' machine. The latest mechanical metaphor for the mind is the computer, the thinking machine, and the model for memory, the holographic, optical, laser storage device. I am sure that as our machines get more and more sophisticated, our mechanical model for the mind will become even more subtle. But stop and think about the computer. Is a computer only a machine? Is it purely mechanical? Does a computer not also have a mind? A computer is, after all, not merely hardware. The most sophisticated hardware cannot function without software. Software is created by human minds inputting design into mechanical formats. Human minds draw their designs from their own programming; from language, culture, education, even the special language of mathematics—all modifications of the influence of other minds. Further, the computer can only provide a result when interpreted by other minds who use the computer. The computer metaphor does not resolve the body/mind problem. It simply translates it into another medium.

Now, neuroscience approaches mind, its analysis, control and modification, as if it were approaching a computer, as hardware. This is true of the radical materialist approach that Dr. Potter championed in the earlier dialogue.[20] It is a powerful approach. If a computer has no hard disk, it will have no memory; if it has a huge disk, it will have a huge memory. Its CPU, central processing unit, will determine how much data it can process, how quickly and so forth. But none of its hardware components can do a thing, no matter how elaborate, no matter how much current goes through them, if the energies are not directed by software, the design that gives pattern and structure. But does neuroscience approach the need for software? Who is working on the software? Are the cognitive sciences avoiding the software problem so as not to be dismissed as *soft* sciences?

The point is that we need *soft* sciences to deal with the software of the mind. Say the neurosciences could develop the new bionic brain; say they add millions of silicon chips, new CPUs multiplying the brain's connection capacity a billionfold; say they could localize the specific neurons that do this or that function and multiply them all a trillionfold; say they could pump in enriched neurotransmitters and neuromodulators at will; say they could give the experimental subject the potential of multiplying the intelligence, the access to information; say they could provide mechanical access to the entire contents of all the libraries in the world, all the satellite archives, all the microscope and telescope archives. Imagine all this attached to your head. Imagine yourself being the node of consciousness inside such a fantastic knowledge and experience machine. And imagine that all of this is unorganized by any appropriate structuring system of software. Flick on the switch and it would either not access and simply leave you cold, all strapped up in a bunch of wires, or it would blow out all your fuses by overload of random input.

So to be practical, if we were to manage a project to augment the human brain with bionics—the wonderful project Dr. Potter and His Holiness joked about—a project to create a super brain to accomplish all sorts of useful tasks, we would allot a large chunk of the budget to the development of the software for the bionic brain. As Dr. Potter said, a lot of taxpayers' funds, a lot of funds are allotted to the hardware. What funds are allotted to the software? This, we would like to know. We would never spend all our funds on hardware and ignore the development of software if we were managing a bionic brain.

Yet what are we doing as a civilization in the vast, largely unmanaged project of scientific research and development that constitutes our 'progress'? We are putting most of our effort into the hardware. That is why it is so expensive, and that is why it gets so little result. We are like a computer builder who keeps improving his computer in the shop, in design components, in size, in complexity, yet never turns it on, has no program for it and so never gets to use the thing at all. Now why does neuroscience do this? Why does psychology also try to climb into the lap of the hard sciences by clinging to neuroscience, trying to find a relationship by calling them both cognitive science? It is because of the basic philosophical error of metaphysical materialism that our whole culture has made. Western sciences were most recently reborn from the Renaissance revolt against the spiritualism undergirding the oppressive domination of the Church's bureau of dogma and instruments of thought control. As a result, a metaphysical decision was taken and, often unwittingly, maintained, from the seventeenth century to the present, to rule mind out of the natural order and deal with all problems as physical. Twentieth-century philosophy has sealed its own doom by discovering in various ways that philosophy is finished, that exploration of reality is meaningless except as measurement by scientific extensions of the senses. The fact that the decision to view reality as material was a collective decision and not an objective discovery has been forgotten. And this has led to the current dogmatism called scientific materialism.

But dogmatism cripples any science, including psychology, the inner science. Dogmatism ensues where hypothesis hardens into ideology. It puts blinders on the observer, whose narrowed vision overlooks enormous amounts of evidence. And who is challenging this dogmatism of modern science? From within the West, we do not see any credible challenge. Religious fundamentalists have discerned the dogmatic pretensions of scientific theory to absolute truth and they have reverted to prescientific counter-dogmas such as creationism. Liberal humanists have brought up issues of ethics, questioning decisions to conduct experiments and implement technologies without a thorough understanding of the consequences. Governments question the utility of huge basic research experiments at enormous costs with seemingly remote applications. But the fundamentalists lack mainstream credibility, answering one irrationality with another. The humanists can restrain some abuses, but are hamstrung by being steeped in the same materialistic belief system. And governments can only stall developments temporarily since they are always hoping for some eventual military application of whatever results; their greed for scientific progress is too great.

So there is no credible challenge from within our culture, and modern psychology is locked on a course that does not look promising. Thus Tibetan psychology may be just what is vitally needed to provide this challenge. It is not that Tibetan mind science hates materialism and proposes an opposite spiritualism—that would be like the fundamentalist challenge, humanly understandable, yet ineffective. Tibetan science is in fact critical of all dogmatic views, considering any idea erroneous that pretends that it corresponds completely with reality. Materialism is a powerful hypothesis. It is a good base of operation in some contexts, but not so effective in others. Tibetan science has many models of mind and body, not just one. It is aware that all models of reality are in some ways inadequate to convey the inconceivable actuality of things, and so has developed a number of models, different ones to be used for different purposes. This is what His Holiness meant in his answer to the question on mathematics, did mathematics in fact govern things? He said that if you look into things, you will not find anything that you look for. If you look for the referent of any designation you will not find it. And therefore, the referents of designations are only conventionally existent. Now Dr. Matthysse, who asked His Holiness that question, said, when pressed, that he thought that at the end of the chain of symbols and equations there was nothing.[21] But Buddhist philosophy would never agree with that. There is no way that this is nothing. We are simply not nothing, as everyone knows for sure. And what we are is, to be more precise, something that, when we try to pin down what it is, appears to be nothing; yet when we do not try to pin down what it is, looks very much like something. And that is a way of saying that what we are is conventionally, or relatively, existing *some*things, not absolutely existing *some*things. Therefore, any mode of description of the way we are is called conventional, meaning that it is a description that we make up in our intershared mind field, in our field of language. We make it up, we agree with it and over generations we do it, not just here and now. We could not now just set up a convention and decide that all there was in the world was the room that we are in or that the room we are in could fly off to a mountain in Tibet. That would not work because there are millions of others involved in the convention of reality.

This is the Buddhist scientific view. What it means is that every description of reality is conventional and none absolute, and that is why Buddhism can use materialism. Some Buddhists are radical materialists in certain usages, but they are not stuck in that. If they are in another situation, in a situation of ethics, in a situation of psychology, they will not be radical. They will be dualists, or they will be interactionists. Or they can have a flexibility of intellectual view which, in fact, connects very strongly to the notion that hypothesis is awaiting disproof and that science is always open to further dimensions of reality provided by further evidence. Once you are locked into a certain ideological theory, you can only look for certain evidence, you are no longer an open-minded scientist, you will never discover anything really great, and you will never be awarded a Nobel prize. If you understand emptiness and the fact that there is nothing beyond a string of symbols, nothing including nothing, that it is not nothing there but something that can always be redescribed, then your mind will achieve a flexibility where you will have genuine, break-through, eureka experiences because you will be able to review things from other dimensions, as Einstein did, for example, with the dogma of ether, when he discovered relativity. You will not be locked into a particular ideology.

So this is what I mean when I say that Buddhism developed a variety of models of reality, of mind/body relationships, different ones useful for different purposes. To develop an effective system of medicine, it employed a physicalistic, reductionistic model of life, with mind reduced to body. For everyday moral philosophy, it put forth a dualistic model of mind and body and forcefully guarded against the materialistic reductionism that was popular among the playboy merchants of urban India. For the advanced meditational practice of the messianistic, universalistic philosophy of Buddhism, it put forth a unitive, mentalistic model of body/mind unity, where body was reduced to mind. For the most subtle level of philosophy and science, it developed a relativistic, conventionalistic model of mind/body interactionism. And there were numerous permutations of these models.

Now this ideological flexibility is not something new from Tibetan psychology. Western science also upholds the ideal that theory is purely hypothetical, orienting the observer toward a thing or process and sorting out the observations and making them meaningful. If supported by observation, a theory remains only temporarily true, forever awaiting disproof. Tibetan psychology does not add anything new by manifesting that same spirit of flexibility of theory and openness to empirical experience. It reinforces scientific openness. What it does offer that is significant is a method of attention to the mind that is not reductionalistically materialistic, but still is critical, rational, systematic and analytic. This challenge and complement to the dogma of materialism is of crucial importance to the further progress of Western science, particularly psychology.

There is, however, something even more basic and important: What is the purpose of psychology? What human action can become successful if valid knowledge of the psyche is attained? Although knowledge for its own sake has become an unquestioned human good, there is also good reason for taking a science and its corresponding art—in the broadest sense of technology—together. This highlights the resulting human good that can be derived from a particular system of knowledge; each science relates to its corresponding art. Psychology seeks to understand the self, the mind, the inner workings of sensations, perceptions, cognitions, emotions, instincts and so forth. The resulting art should contribute directly to the human capacity for happiness, for creativity, for understanding. Sensation should be better understood in order to foster more pleasurable and elevating sensations. Or if, as Dr. Potter feared with the poor cocaine addicts, there are too many pleasurable sensations, they should be understood in order to tone them down, or to diffuse them into other areas of life; not to lobotomize people to prevent any euphoria, but to channel a bit of euphoria into their everyday interactions. Why should they not be euphoric while carefully doing a scientific experiment? It should not be impossible to be a little euphoric and yet still carefully pour from one beaker to another in the laboratory.

Perceptions and cognitions should be improved and made more

accurate and reliable. Emotions should be studied with the greatest care, to learn how to diminish those that make us unhappy and increase those that make us happy. Their effect on the health of the body should be studied and those with bad effects diminished and those with good effects increased. Is not this, after all, the dream of neuroscience? If human inner workings can be reduced to observable, repeatable, controllable and manipulable quanta of chemical, electrical or other energies in the brain, then the human mind will at last have become controllable and improvable. This lures the scientists, engages their supporters and frightens the humanists. When we hear the modern drug-oriented psychologist rejoice in antidepressants, antipsychotics, tranquilizers and so forth, are they not underlining the real purpose of psychology; the precise understanding and benevolent modification of human mental states so as to ameliorate human behavior and thus the quality of life for the individual and society? The result we want to produce here is subjective. Happiness is subjective, finally. Only you know directly, only you can observe immediately, when you are happy. You do depend on outer conditions to some degree, but the central subjective events of sensations, emotions, interpretations, cognitions are the direct causes of the central subjective results of happiness and unhappiness. To seek to generate these central results only through the root of manipulating peripheral conditions is clumsy at best, ineffective at worst. The central task of culture using language, story, myth, ritual, story, ethics, religion, philosophy, art, landscape and whatever else, is to create inner-directed persons who feel a culturally-driven impulse to participate in society, to contribute to it creatively and to restrain negative impulses that tear the social fabric. When cultures lose the ability to do this, and try to impose order by outside methods—law, police force, institutional thought control, compulsory physical regimes such as behavioral trainings, drugs, diet and such like—the results are always disappointing and the society eventually collapses. As this has long been the experience of human societies, why should psychology purposely ignore the study of human inner workings? Why should it find them inaccessible, incomprehensible, useless and meaningless? Is it not thereby depriving itself of its very *raison d'être*, its own distinctive, constituted area as a science? Early on in Western psychology, inner states were taken with some seriousness, but with psychologists more and more concerned to fit into the ranks of 'hard' scientists, inner states became less and less important, finally being ruled out altogether as illusory, inaccessible, powerless and useless.

So modern psychologists find themselves less and less empowered to understand and help people through their own inner channels. The dysfunctional person may sometimes have a physical problem that can be dealt with by physical medicine, but most often they have problems in their inner world, problems in the software that drives their mind/body complex in inadequate ways. They are imprisoned within distorted ideologies, poisoned by negative emotions, irritated and frightened by warped perceptions and paralyzed by self-defeating habits. But the psychologist is given no time or license or facility to deal with these problems directly. He or she cannot get to the bottom of this problem with each patient. Only a few élite patients with sufficient time and resources can have such depth analytic treatment. The majority are put into provisional control situations with artificial asylum environments and drugs to dull the stresses. In this environment, the problem is only put in stasis with little hope of improvement and great expectation of deterioration. It is rather like taking a malfunctioning computer with a software problem, lubricating it, warehousing it, adding new hardware components and so forth, all without any software analysis and modification.

Now here is where the Tibetan psychological traditions can make a vital contribution. With its sophisticated methods of software analysis and modification, it can help with the individual's inner reprogramming. Its analytic method is incorporated in an immense literature describing the workings of the mind and a dazzling variety of conceptual systems for coping with it. There is a vast array of arts or mental technologies, modification techniques that enable individuals to incorporate and integrate the improved software. This is the broad array of meditational practices. But meditation by itself cannot accomplish the job. It must be supported from below, so to speak, by a solidly ethical life-style that generates a minimum of disturbance for the individual and his or her associates and a maximum of harmony and supportive energy, and it must be guided from above by understanding, by intelligent programming through realistic views or orientations, what the Buddhists call wisdom.

His Holiness sketched examples of the reprogramming task required to transform a human biocomputer's operation driven by anger and hate into an operation guided by patience and love. He mentioned overcoming the innate, naive absolutism that makes us cling to our conceptual structurings of reality and so come into conflict with others who do not agree with them, and giving rise to greed and anger over it. This is a reprogramming task on the level of an educational process that employs contemplative methods.

I would like to introduce two other examples of reprogramming from the tantric technology, one on the level of medical practice and the other on the level of transcendental contemplation.

The first is the discipline of medical diagnosis through what is called the nerve channel examination. The trained Tibetan doctor develops a combination of memorization, anatomical learning, subtle visualization and contemplative heightening of sensitivity. He or she trains the six tip corners of the first three fingers of each hand to be attuned to twelve channels of communication from the patient's body. Placing these fingers anywhere on the body of the patient, but preferably on the radial arteries of the two wrists, the doctor becomes a psychic CAT-scan machine. He or she lets the awareness enter into the body of the patient, travel through the blood, lymph and neural systems into various organs and vessels, and emerge with a detailed picture of the exact physical condition of the patient's body. This is thought to be mysterious and perhaps mystical by both its fans and its skeptics. But we do not need to go into mysticism or spiritualism, we can understand it simply as a kind of sophisticated biocomputer programming. Just as an EEG puts electrodes on a scalp and measures various functions within a patient's brain and body, so a specially programmed human nervous system touches the patient's body— these fingers become like electrodes—and gets specific vibration patterns it is attuned to receive. Simultaneously, it activates an elaborate interpretation program, which correlates its readings with specific functions and malfunctions within the patient's body. The twelve sensors in the fingers are mentally programmed to sense a pulse or vibration from heart, lung, liver and so on. The Tibetan doctor is in fact visualizing himself and the patient as purely material, elemental processes. So there is no mystic idea of mind involved in this case. A Tibetan doctor is insulted when patients come to him or her, as Westerners sometimes do in India, and expect some sort of spiritual lecture. He says, 'I'm here for your physical problem, not for a spiritual lecture.' So they use materialistic reductionism in this context. They simply turn their body and mind, by a long training that takes twenty-five years, into a kind of CAT-scan. This is the 'wetware' and these are the electrodes. Like a very sensitive musician or a skilled masseur, they can feel what is going on inside the person.

Now, Western medicine cannot understand the remarkable diagnostic results a skilled Tibetan physician can get with the attention concentrated through this imaginative program. The Western researcher assumes that the Tibetan thinks that each organ somehow has a telegraph-like wire connected to the spot on the wrist, some sort of primitive notion of anatomy. But that is not correct. The Tibetans do not consider that there is some sort of wire going from the liver to some place on the wrist, they simply do not. What it is is simply a software program.

When a lie-detector reads an external energy fluctuation as evidence of an inner lie, a sense of tension deep in the mind, guilt, a furtive concept, it is not necessary for there to be a wire from the little energy pattern of the neuron where the mental image is to go from the network of synapses to some place on the skin where the electrode is. The machine is programmed through electrodes to detect extremely subtle interior pattern differences from coarse potential differences on the surface. Similarly, the physician has a mental model of the mind/body complexes of both physician and patient. He has memorized a complex set of metaphors for the different types of pulses; like the sound of the cuckoo, like water dripping in spring, like a crippled bird hopping and staggering and so forth. He or she feels them under one or another finger corner.

Richard Seltzer, MD, gives a remarkable description of Dr. Yeshe Donden, a Tibetan physician, as he read the pulse of a patient at Yale Hospital, which description was made famous by Ram Dass in his wonderful book *How Can I Help?* I will cite some of it because it conveys the picture:[22]

> At last he takes her hand, raising it in both of his own. Now he bends over the bed in a kind of crouching stance, his head drawn down into the collar of his robe. His eyes are closed as he feels for her pulse. In a moment he has found the spot and for the next half hour he remains thus: suspended above the patient like some exotic golden bird with folded wings, holding the pulse of the woman beneath his fingers, cradling her hand in his. All the power of the man seems to have been drawn into this one purpose. It is palpa-

tion of the pulse raised to the state of ritual. From the foot of the bed where I stand, it is as though he and the patient have entered a special place of isolation, of apartness about which a vacancy hovers and across which no violation is possible. From time to time she raises her head to look at the strange figure above her then sinks back once more. I cannot see their hands joined in a correspondence that is exclusive, intimate, his fingertips receiving the voice of her sick body through the rhythm and throb she offers at her wrist. All at once I am envious, not of him, not of Yeshe Donden for his gift of beauty and holiness, but of her, I want to be held like that, touched so, received, and I know that I, who have palpated a hundred thousand pulses, have not felt a single one.

Software of linguistic and pictorial imagination programming creates a human sensing machine that can detect tiny differences in interior organs that reveal a symptomatology. The differences are interpreted through a memorized text that encodes thousands of years of accumulated experience by highly accomplished physicians. The interpretations are themselves connected to other memorized texts of codified diagnostic rules, also systematically developed. This is cross-referenced and checked with data and interpretation from visual examination of the patient, including their body surfaces, eyes and tongue; and a sophisticated testing of the urine, systematically analyzed in terms of color, smell, taste, bubble formation patterns, visible secretions, viscosity and so on,[23] and from a textually guided process of detailed interrogation. The result is a remarkably reliable system of diagnosis, all without hardware machines to extend the senses, and all without a pursuit of microanalysis into the inner space of the cellular or atomic levels to such a fine degree that it is almost impossible to bring the results of the analysis into an interpretation that relates effectively to the person as a whole. I cannot give an exhaustive discussion of this diagnostic software program. I am only trying to suggest a new way of looking at it and studying it, perhaps with a view to adapting it for the training of modern physicians who base their interpretations on such a huge mass of data that they have great difficulty in coordinating that mass with the growth life process of the patient.

My second example is the *gTum-mo* meditation, which Herbert Benson has studied. I want to present this from the interior point of view. There is a sophisticated visualization program implemented by the yogi or yogini who practices *gTum-mo*, the yoga of channeled

1. A typical multi-armed deity, the Kalachakra. Cultivating a physical self-image with such arms and legs is a subliminal method of awakening the sensitivity of the central nervous system.

furor that can direct intense heat to generate specific desired inner experiences.

This extremely subtle programming employs a series of solidly stabilized and vividly focused, visualized images. The yogi or yogini melts the self image of the habitual coarse body by reviewing its ultimate voidness. Then, he or she revises the inner model of the nervous system. In pictures we see this yogi wearing his spacesuit for the measurement. But where is his mind, and what is the inner geography? What is going on in the subtlest level of the control mechanism of that yogi's body, seen as a mechanism that is producing heat? In order to understand this we have to know about the software. This is what I will now describe, in very brief compass.

The yogi melts the self-image of the habitual coarse body by reviewing its ultimate voidness. This means that the yogi has to be someone who has had some degree of the visceral experience of emptiness. He or she has had the experience of the structure of self completely melting away and has actually discovered viscerally what Dr. Matthysse referred to as the lack of anything at the end of the symbol train. The train of symbols of 'I', the train of 'myself', this body, these two arms, has gone beyond the subatomic atoms of this body, gone to where all of that has dissolved and he has viscerally experienced it through the critical meditation on emptiness. So that yogi or yogini can dissolve at will the sense of identifying with this ordinary kind of human coarse body. He or she then revises the inner model, and does not leave it in the state of dissolvedness, in some sort of blankness.

First, he or she visualizes the body and environment as a symbolic, archetypal or deity manifestation in a pure mandala setting. There are a great variety of these embodiments and environments, which are well known from the paintings of Tibetan archetype deities; the Tibetan paintings of those deities with many faces, many arms or many legs in complicated postures and so forth (see Fig. 1). These deities are not just spirits to be invoked and worshipped with some mumbo-jumbo. That is not the point at all. They are models of the self that can be used to achieve certain specific states of mind, certain special sensibilities. When one has dissolved the coarse model of self as this two-armed, one-headed being into voidness, one re-arises in the form of a multi-headed, multi-armed being for the purpose of having a different feeling. Imagine how it would feel if, in your central nervous system, instead of only two arms you had hundreds of arms. There would be this feeling of reaching out, of tremendous energy through all these arms. It is a way of structuring that feeling in the inner nervous system by visualizing that form of the outer body. We could not do that with our entrenched sense of naive identification with this body. We must first have realized emptiness and dissolved this; only then can we imaginatively reconstruct it.

After the yogi or yogini has visualized an archetype body, they then leave even this coarse deity body, ignore the outer embodiment and environment, the mandala, and re-envision the mind/body complex as a kind of living machine, or biocomputer, consisting of channels in a specific network of patterns, a neural network, energies

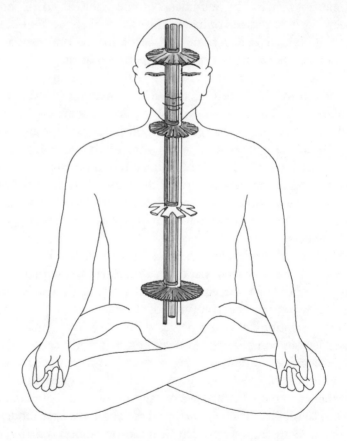

2. A simplified diagram of the chakra system showing the three central channels upon which a yogi or yogini meditates during *gTum-mo*.

3. The subtle nervous system of the yogi: energy rising from the seed syllable at the heart chakra to the HAM in the crown chakra, melts the coarse awareness drops and energy impulses into freedoms and blisses.

moving in particular ways and biochemical drops or nodes of subtle awarenesses, drops as foci of awareness or seed cells. This is the tantric area that interfaces with neuroscience mentioned by His Holiness. This machine looks like a sort of gyroscope with flower wheels at five or so levels along a central tube, the petals of the wheels branching out into the whole nervous system (see Fig. 2).

The practitioner no longer thinks about any kind of arms or legs or appendages but just becomes a kind of tube, a neural net tube, like a computer that is set up with its wires connected in a tube. Once that visualization is stable and vivid, the yogi or yogini can initiate the procedure of furor fire by visualizing an awareness drop in the shape of a white, blazing-hot letter AH, just a squiggle at a specific point in the network mechanism—usually in the central column at the level of the flower wheel, or flower center, below the navel of the coarse body (see Fig. 3). In the center of the body, one visualizes this blazing white-hot letter AH. Subtle wind energies are directed at that blazing AH as the breath goes in the nostrils. This, remember, is not an ordinary coarse body, so the breath entering the nostrils is visualized as going down two tubes on two sides and projecting energy that then blows across the AH and fans it like fanning a flame with bellows, making it spark and intensifying the heat. Then the AH blazes up intensely. Eventually it makes the entire inside of this biomechanical computer molten and aglow, melting all vestiges of coarse awareness drops and energy impulses into freedoms and blisses, dissolving everything into the subtle dimension of the central column.

Now this yogi is someone who would be highly immune to cocaine addiction, because when he or she goes into that tube function, the idea is to have an intense bliss or euphoria all up and down the central nervous system. This is also the reason why in Tibetan tantric art you see sexual imagery, because the intensity of blisses that are experienced in this *gTum-mo* melting process is considered to be a million times that of sexual orgasm. It is not that tantra is a way of improving sex. Tantra is not needed to have sex in the East; people have it quite naturally and easily. The reason for the sexual imagery in Tantra is that it provides a hint of the kind of bliss or euphoria generated to suffuse the entire system through the furor fire.

This is what the *gTum-mo* yogi is doing. The melting of sheets is a peripheral manifestation, a kind of macho outer sign of working on the inner level. The real function is on the inner level to focus the winds and melt the drops into blisses. Then one does not lose one's mind in the blisses but one uses the blisses to generate love and compassion for all beings, to deepen one's wisdom about emptiness, to energize one's feeling of universal responsibility and to send out rays of love and compassion to everyone in the whole planet. That is what this biomechanism is doing. It is like a kind of *mani*-wheel,[24] a living biocomputer *mani*-wheel, that wants to send out OM MANI PADME HUM—'Hail the Jewel in the Lotus!'—send out rays of love to the whole universe. It is a subjective visualization, but still it is the core radiation at the heart of Tibetan culture.

Then the melting process registers subjectively as a rehearsal of the dissolving process of normal death and the yogi or yogini enters into a sequence of inner experiential realms of the subtle and extremely subtle minds, as they are called, eventually immersing him or herself into what is known as the clear light of universal freedom, or clear light of absolute voidness. This again is not the end goal, because the voidness, clear light mind is here right now. It is the essence of all of our being right now, of everyone here right now. But here the yogi or yogini goes into it fully and experientially, and knows what this reality really is. And then the final goal is to bring that non-duality into every aspect of daily life so that one becomes a walking manifestation of clear light, absolute voidness and great bliss. One is love and compassion in every gesture. This is why the Dalai Lama has such a wonderful feeling about him and why it feels so empty when he leaves; because he is a master of this tradition.

After much practice of this process, the yogi or yogini supposedly develops a subtle micro-understanding of the life process itself, which enables him or her to engineer genetically the buddha forms required to communicate bliss and freedom to other beings. The coarse heat and temperature differences read by thermal instruments on the surface of such a yogi's body are the coarse by-products of the inner furor fire process, the main aim of which is the evolutionary acceleration sketched out above. The point of the example here today is to see how the Tibetan inner technology uses visualization to create software programming for the biocomputer's wetware that can lead to extraordinary results. Without subscribing to such exalted pictures as the attainment of Buddhahood and so on, we can provisionally imagine that designed implementations of such visualized patterns could be used for healing, for repatterning neural malfunctions, or for pre-patterning neural superfunctions.

Finally, the practical recommendations emerging from this thesis and these examples are that, in the ongoing dialogue between the Tibetan and the Western mind science traditions, it is crucial that we put as much effort into discovering Tibetan psychology's software resources as we do into measuring the exterior of the Tibetan body. To do that we have to strengthen Tibetan institutions, we have to encourage the study of these yogas by Tibetans themselves. If we do it in this way, then I am sure that we will succeed in something very creative.

5

Cognition: A Western Perspective

Howard E. Gardner, Ph.D
Professor of Education, Harvard University

Cognition:
A Western Perspective

In this overview I am going to focus on what one might call *hard* cognition—thinking, intelligence, rationality. I will not talk much about other aspects of mind, such as feeling, emotions, spirit, will and consciousness.[25] I seek to convey the sweep of views in the West, one might say from Socrates to cybernetics or from Plato to parallel distributed processing. In casting around for a way to do it I remembered a movie I saw recently—*Mr. & Mrs. Bridge*. In it, events representing different decades were designated by individual snapshots. For those people for whom the snapshots were evocative it was possible to quickly get a feeling for a significant period of time. So I have identified seven pivotal moments in Western intellectual history, and I am going to give you some images to help you get a feeling for each moment. I will also identify six themes that pervade the Western view of the mind. I will conclude by mentioning five ways of thinking that might actually cut across the East-West divide.

Snapshot One: The Meno

Snapshot number one goes back 2,500 years to the time of Socrates and in particular to a dialogue called the *Meno*. In this dialogue, Socrates talks to a slave boy and proceeds to show that, even though the slave boy at first appears to be ignorant, in fact he knows all of geometry and just about everything else, as well. The reason he knows everything is because he was born with all that knowledge. Unfortunately he has forgotten it, so Socrates has to ask him questions to remind him. This image posits mind as recall, a very powerful, recurrent image in the West.

The *Meno* is also important, however, because from my point of view, it set the Western philosophical agenda till today. What is knowledge? Where does it come from? How is it accessed? How is it represented? That is what the study of hard cognition in philosophy, psychology and, more recently, in cognitive science, has been for the last 2,500 years.

Snapshot Two: The Birth of Modern Epistemology

We are now going to speed forward in the snapshots 2,000 years to the late Renaissance, the beginning of the Enlightenment, the time of the great philosophers, Descartes, Locke, Berkeley and Kant. These thinkers developed what Richard Rorty[26] calls the 'mind idea'—the idea that there is a separate realm called the mind, which has its own rules of functioning. The mind, according to Rorty, is a mirror of nature, a way of finding out what nature is like and of reflecting that state to you.

Now, Descartes shared in common with the classical philosophers a belief that ideas are basically innate and that you are born knowing how to think and it is this act of thinking that confirms your existence. But the next generation of philosophers, the empiricists, had an opposing claim. In their view, you are born knowing nothing, as a blank slate, and the mirror of nature is acquired through experience over the course of your life. Kant tried to synthesize these points of view by recognizing the importance of experience but by saying there was something about our cognitive apparatus that *made* us apprehend experience in a certain way. We could not help but think in terms of time and number and causality.

Snapshot Three: A Science of Mind

Snapshot three takes us into science, which is supposed to be a step beyond philosophy. Newton and Galileo gave us physics, so to speak; Lavoisier, chemistry; and Darwin was the principal figure in biology in the nineteenth century. In their wake, it was virtually inevitable that psychology would come to be created as a scientific discipline, a discipline that styled itself, to some extent, after biology, but really more after physics.

One basic notion was to think about the mind as obeying psychophysical laws, which in a sense mimicked the kinds of physical laws that Newton and Galileo had laid out. One sought to measure the speed and the accuracy of mental processes like remembering, forgetting, perceiving, attending and the like. That is what academic psychology is really about: creating laboratory situations with brass instruments where you can measure these mental processes the way physicists conduct experiments in a cloud chamber.

And, if you look in most psychology textbooks, you will not see in the index most of the topics discussed at this symposium, because they are seen as being outside the realm of academic psychology. The extreme of academic psychology, as you know, is behaviorism, which tried to measure as few things as possible with the hope that they would apply to as many diverse processes and as many diverse species as possible; at the same time behaviorism sought to exorcise any talk about mind ideas, mental representation, the brain and the like.

Snapshot Four: Measuring Intelligence

I want now to mention some exceptions, and to introduce some new entries in this mental slide show. A first event occurred around 1900, when the first intelligence test was created. At that time in France, the leaders of the educational establishment were trying to predict who would have trouble in school. They asked a man named Alfred Binet to create some kind of an instrument. Binet got the clever idea of giving people lots of questions and seeing which ones were passed by people who did well in school and which ones failed by people who did not do well in school. Almost without knowing it, he had created the first intelligence test.

An intelligence test is important because, for many people, it represents what psychology is all about. Psychologists figure out how smart you are, and the IQ test is a kind of spiffy, quick way of ascertaining the speed and flexibility of your thinking. The intelligence test is very much with us even today. Most of us deep down believe that there is a certain thing in our mind that is *how smart we are*, and that psychologists and neurologists could figure it out if they knew exactly where to place the electrodes. So that is one corner of academic psychology, along with a view of the mind as a kind of speed and flexibility machine.

Snapshot Five: Mind as Unconscious

Freud's epic *Interpretation of Dreams* was published in the same year that the first IQ test was invented. Freud had a view of the mind as being submerged, unconscious, heavily censorious. The Freudian perspective is probably the aspect of soft psychology that has made its way most prominently into the popular ethos.

So we have gone from the philosophy of 2,500 years ago to the philosophy of a few hundred years ago to a set of milestones in more recent psychology: the brass instruments, the mind as a speedy, flexible kind of instrument, and the mind as submerged and largely not accessible to consciousness.

Snapshot Six: The Cognitive Revolution

In September 1956, the cognitive revolution began. That date is actually recognized, with a certain amount of tongue in cheek, by historians as the time when behaviorism was, so to speak, overthrown; when IQ was recognized as being entirely applied and atheoretical; and when the unconscious processes and the notion that a lot of mind was not accessible to introspection and reflection were called into question within the broader behavioral science community.[27]

The reason why September 1956 is singled out is because there was an important meeting at the Massachusetts Institute of Technology. Scientists like Herbert Simon, Noam Chomsky, Alan Newell and George Miller put forth the idea that it was okay again in the behavioral sciences to think about mind, to think about thinking, to think about reasoning, to think about problem solving. The reason it was now okay was revealing. We now had computers that did this sort of thing. If computers could think and reason, then it was really a shame to withhold those abilities from human beings, even though much of behaviorism had got a lot of mileage by observing that kind of constraint. These are probably the three core disciplines in the cognitive sciences: psychology, linguistics and artificial intelligence; but philosophy, anthropology and neuroscience are also important.

Well, what did the cognitive revolution hold? What did it entail? There was a mainstream view up to around 1980. I claim that basically, if you are a 'card-carrying' cognitivist, you probably believe in the following five things:

1) The Western philosophical agenda, dating back to Plato, is important. We do care about what knowledge is, where it comes from, how it is accessed, transformed and the like. These may not be questions in other parts of the world, but they are very important questions in the West.

2) Second is the notion of what is called a representational level. The idea here is a little bit complicated, but I will try to simplify. Between the *neuronal level*—the wetwear that you can touch or at least look at under microscopes—and the *cultural level*—the notion that there are different cultures with histories and practices and so on—there is a third level of analysis. We call this intermediate level the *representational level*. This level cannot be touched or seen but it is believed to exist in the head. It entails the notion that we have and use schemata, scripts, ideas, symbol systems and other cognate kinds of mental entities. If you are a cognitivist, you believe it is legitimate to study the representational level.

3) The third belief is that the computer is central. Not only do all cognitive scientists use computers in their own work, but they also believe that the computer is the best model of the human mind, and many believe that the human mind is a computer of one sort or another.

4) The remaining two features are of a negative sort. Cognitivists prefer not to have to take into account the *context* in which a behavior or thought takes place. The context is seen as a slippery slope; once one begins to take into account contextual factors, there is no way of knowing when to stop. And so cognitivists prefer to study mental elements and operations in as pure a form as possible, disregarding the social or cultural context in so far as possible.

5) The final feature involves a parallel inclination to avoid the *affective* side of experience. Here, different motives are at work. In some instances, cognitivists believe that affect falls outside of their purview; in some cases, they feel that affective considerations are not that important altogether; and sometimes cognitivists recognize

the necessity of dealing with affective considerations but simply feel that they are too difficult to 'factor in' at the present time. In this last instance, the motive is similar to the motive for ignoring context: do not make the scientific task any more difficult than necessary.

Those are the five precepts that exemplify the cognitive science of 1980. But it is now 1991, and these have all been called into question. The most interesting re-examination for me, because it is what I work on myself, is the critique of the notion that the mind is a single kind of apparatus that can be tested, say, by a single kind of test that probes general intelligence.

Snapshot Seven: Mind as Pluralistic

In all the disciplines in cognitive science over the last ten or fifteen years, there has been a real challenge to the univocal view of the mind. Many people believe that the mind is pluralistic, it is composed of a number of mental organs, or computational devices, or information processing mechanisms. These devices may all function on a kind of equal level, with none of them having hierarchy over any others.

Let me try to make this concrete. I will use an example from our own work, in what is called the theory of multiple intelligences.[28] This theory is a critique of the Binet notion that there is a single thing called intelligence that can be readily measured either through paper or pencil or with some kind of electrophysiological probe.

With my colleagues over the years, looking at a lot of sources of information about human beings in different cultures, we came up with the notion that human beings are better thought of as having seven different kinds of intelligence. All people have all of the intelligences, but people differ in the kinds of profiles of intelligence they have. They probably differ for genetic reasons, because of the nature of the culture in which they live, because of their interests, their parents, their teachers and the accidents of life.

I define intelligence as the ability to solve a problem or to fashion a product, to make something. In an IQ test you cannot test whether anybody can make anything because you have only about sixty items and thirty minutes to finish the test. But whether you can write a symphony, choreograph a dance, run a meeting, do therapy or meditate successfully—these are products that are valued in at least one culture. In defining intelligence in terms of cultural value, I am saying something radical from a psychological perspective. If we really believe that it is possible to up the head, stick in an electrode and find out how smart somebody is, then it should not matter what culture they are in. But I believe the opposite. I believe that the whole notion of intelligence is incoherent absent from a particular cultural context in which you can express, develop or realize whatever proclivities you may have.

So that is a working definition of intelligence. Now here is a list of intelligences that my colleagues and I believe that we have discovered. Each intelligence is introduced by a portrait of an individual who exemplifies that intelligence.

1. *Linguistic intelligence*. VIRGINIA WOOLF exemplifies linguistic intelligence. A person gifted with linguistic intelligence is one who thinks naturally in terms of language and is able to use language flexibly and productively. Poets, novelists, lawyers, orators, all are linguistically intelligent.

2. *Logical-mathematical intelligence*. In our century EINSTEIN epitomizes logical-mathematical intelligence. As the name implies, logicians, mathematicians, and scientists operate by acting upon certain kinds of quantitative and implicative symbols. Piaget, the great Swiss psychologist, thought that he was studying all of intelligence, but I maintain that he was focused on this variety in particular.

3. *Musical intelligence*. Musical intelligence is directly analogous to linguistic intelligence. Just as some individuals 'think' in linguistic terms, others think in musical forms. LEONARD BERNSTEIN is a recent instance of a musically intelligent person. One can call this a talent, provided that one also calls language a talent.

4. *Spatial intelligence*. Individuals who are spatially intelligent, like PABLO PICASSO, are able to form spatial models of the proximal and/or distal worlds, and to operate readily on those models. A variety of societal roles, ranging from sculptor to sailor to surgeon, all depend upon highly-developed spatial intelligence.

5. *Bodily-kinesthetic intelligence*. In our century, MARTHA GRAHAM has come to symbolize the use of one's body to solve problems or to

fashion a product. Dancers, but also athletes, actors, craftspeople, surgeons and technicians, all have skilled bodily intelligence.

6. *Interpersonal intelligence*. My final forms of intelligence have to do with the realm of human beings. Interpersonal intelligence denotes the capacity to understand other individuals, to work well with them, to motivate them. People in public life like MARTIN LUTHER KING exhibit unusual interpersonal intelligence, as do teachers, therapists, actors, salespeople, and religious and political leaders.

7. *Intrapersonal intelligence*. While the interpersonal intelligence looks outward, intrapersonal intelligence involves a correlative understanding of oneself: one's strengths, weaknesses, desires, fears and the capacity to use this knowledge to make judicious decisions about how to lead one's life. FREUD is a person who helped many individuals, including himself, achieve better self-insight.

Having introduced the idea of a plurality of intelligences, I now want to do two other things and will then conclude. First of all, I want to talk about some themes that I think have pervaded the Western view of the mind, which I also believe are being challenged nowadays, from both within and outside the Western tradition. The first notion of modern Western thought is that the mind is very *individual-centered*. You study the individual; from Descartes on, that has been the model. But many people are beginning to appreciate the social aspect of mind, that mind is in many ways not just in yourself but in other people, in the human resources around you. People study teams of workers in offices, in factories, on a boat, working with computers. It turns out that the intelligence is not exclusively in the person's head, it is in all the heads working together, and people depend upon other heads to do other things. So we are moving a little bit away from the individual as the sole center of the study of mind.

The second point is a focus on *rationality of a logical-mathematical sort*, a very dominant Western theme. Many people—for example the well-known psychologist Jerome Bruner, one of the fathers of the cognitive revolution—now talk about other modes of mind, such as the *narrative mode*, which is important but does not work in the same way as the logical mode. And I myself, as the list of intelligences conveyed, am interested in artistic modes of thinking, which are also quite different from the logical-rational. In no way is what a Martha

Graham does, what a Stravinsky does, or what a Virginia Woolf does inferior to or worse than what an Einstein does. It is simply different. It is a different way of solving problems, fashioning products and finding problems.

So a third point is that the focus has shifted from *problem solving to making something and to problem finding*. Some people think that you can get computers to recreate scientific discoveries. However, so far when that has been done, the problems, the data have already been given to the computer. The whole trick in discoveries of any sort is to figure out what the problem is and which data are relevant. This is much harder to do, but it is beginning to interest people.

The fourth point is in *allegiance to the scientific method*. The scientific method, of course, changes over time. The scientific method is groping in this century for a much more flexible way of thinking about what science is and of ascertaining the kinds of data relevant to science and the kinds of methods that people use. Reductionism is one way, but there are systems theories and cybernetics, and many more people doing case studies and even introspective studies than would have been the case forty or fifty years ago.

A fifth point, which relates to the first point, is that we used to think that intelligence occurred completely in the head but we now realize that *intelligence is distributed*. If we take away your books and your computers and your files and your notebooks, you will become a dummy. In fact you are close to a blank slate, because so much of human intelligence consists in the artifacts as well as the other people with whom we deal. An interest in how people develop a system of thinking with portfolios, journals, record-keeping, and various kinds of hardware and software represents another happy shift in the view of mind.

Finally, in my definition I noted that in the West, as part of the hardcore cognitive view, we really have downplayed emotional, motivational and spiritual matters. However, I think that cognitivists are getting bolder, more audacious, less intimidated. They are already beginning to look at some of the things that we might in an earlier time have called hopelessly Eastern, or, perhaps, hopelessly 'West Coast'.

I want to end by mentioning a topic I know absolutely nothing about, and that is *consciousness*. One of the fascinating trends in the last ten years or so has been the number of cognitivists, scientists and rationalists who have become interested in consciousness, both in a computational sense—that is, how you model consciousness with various kinds of computational systems—and in the phenomenal aspects of consciousness. How do we think about that?

Let me mention five different ways in which people are thinking about this. The first, is what I would call the reductionist way. This is basically the notion that there is absolutely nothing special about consciousness. As soon as we understand the neurons we will know all that there is to know. That certainly is the dominant view among scientists and it may well be the right one, but it is a reductionist view that will not be popular with those who are spiritually inclined.

A second point of view is the notion of two different realms. There is the realm of consciousness, which is the realm of experience, and there is the realm of matter, which science tries to explain. Einstein had a wonderful line. He said that the purpose of chemistry is not to recreate the taste of the soup. You could know all that was possible to know about the soup but you would still never know what it tasted like. Similarly, if you are interested in taste, you should read Proust, not medical and physical journals.

A third approach is the notion that yes, we can explain consciousness scientifically but it is going to require an entirely new science. This, I take it, is what Roger Penrose is saying in his new book, *The Emperor's New Mind*.

The fourth way, which is usually how I would conclude, is the ecumenical way. This maintains that we should make use of all the knowledge we can, make use of all the disciplines we can and make use of all the experiences we can. We should learn about consciousness from art as well as from science, we should learn about it from computers but also from reading Proust or Virginia Woolf and by looking at Picasso's paintings. We should pay attention to human intelligence as well as to artificial intelligence. We should pay attention to what is in the East as well as to what is in the West. I take it that this is completely noncontroversial, but it is also somewhat vacuous. And so I am going to conclude with something that is perhaps a shade less vacuous, which I will call ecumenicism with a twist, or perhaps even ecumenicism with mutual shaping. What do I mean by that?

This thought was prompted by the earlier dialogue. There were many interesting things said about actions, states, processes, kinds of explanations and the like. However, in mutual shaping the question is not simply, do you talk to each other?, but rather, do you actually affect the way in which the two speakers think about things? Do you actually seek to restructure people's beliefs, and do you restructure their actions? I would say that a full-blown exploration of mind and consciousness occurs when the participants of a symposium like this not only speak and listen to each other, but actually put their own views at risk. And they say, 'There is something that the sciences are saying' on the one hand, or, 'There is something that the meditators are saying' on the other. 'There is something that might actually make me think differently about things, and go about my daily practice differently.' If that happens, then we will have entered into a genuine dialogue, where the ultimate outcome remains open. And if the dialogue proceeds well, the final synthesis will be greater than, and different from, what any of the participants initially brought to the table.

6

Tibetan and Western Models of Mental Health

Daniel Goleman, Ph.D
Contributing Writer, The New York Times

6

Tibetan and Western Models of Mental Health

It was as a graduate student at Harvard that I first became interested in the notion of Tibetan and other Eastern models of mental health. I was fortunate enough to have a pre-doctoral Harvard Travelling Fellowship, and then a post-doctoral fellowship, that allowed me to live in Asia for two years and study something that, frankly, astounded me when I first realized what was there to be studied.

As a student of psychology at Harvard, I had come to assume, as is the tacit assumption in the West, that psychology is a scientific topic that originated in America and Europe within the last century. So, when I got to Asia and really started to look into Eastern systems of thought, I was astounded to find that cradled within every great religious tradition there is a psychological system, the esoteric part of the religion. And of those systems that I studied, it seemed to me that Tibetan Buddhism contained perhaps the most sophisticated such psychology. It has, for example, a precise phenomenological model and detailed analyses of mental states and the processes of cognition and consciousness. It offers an operational definition of mental health—which I will now share with you—and a method for transforming consciousness that is quite unique and very different from our own approach in the West. And, most significantly, it offers a vision of human possibility that holds that the attainment of states such as equanimity and compassion—that is, a love without attachment—is not just some abstract goal, but possible.

I contend that the model of mental health one finds in Eastern psychologies—and Tibetan Buddhism is the example *par excellence*—really overreaches and extends, in a very powerful way, our own notion of mental health. What intrigues me is that I was never told a thing about this in my graduate training or in any psychology course, although these psychologies have been applied for more than two thousand years. I think that is quite shocking: two thousand years is a long time. Behaviorism should last so long! Cognitive science should last so long, for that matter.

There is a panoply of inner sciences in Tibetan Buddhism. I would like to focus on one of the most elementary. It is a model of the mind shared with other branches of Buddhism—Theravada has a very similar model. It is called Abhidharma.[29] The basic unit of analysis in the Abhidharma model is a single moment of mind in the succession of such moments in the stream of awareness. In this model, each such moment is seen to be characterized by different, if you will, 'flavors', called mental factors. Each mental factor has unique properties that determine our subjective experience from moment to moment. In this model, what is seen as primary in shaping experience is not the external reality—not what is cognized, not the *object* of awareness— but rather the properties of that moment of mind itself. For instance, if the object of awareness is your tax return you could be seeing it through the lens of a mental factor of fear, of anger, of sadness, or, theoretically, of joy—unlikely, however.

The point is that each mental state, each moment of mind, is composed of a shifting array of properties that combine to flavor and define that state. There is a nice pithy Zen saying that makes the point:

> To her lover, a beautiful women is a delight; to an ascetic, a distraction; to a wolf, a good meal.

There are innumerable properties of mind, and how you cut the pie is rather arbitrary. Abhidharma selects fifty or so mental factors as being crucial, roughly half of which are considered unhealthy, or un- wholesome, most of the others being considered healthy, or whole- some.

The rule of thumb for mental health is very straightforward. Those states that are unhealthy, or unwholesome, are those that are not conducive to calm, to tranquility, to equilibrium, to meditation, to the attainment of enlightenment. That is a basic rule in this psycho- logical system. If a mental factor maintains or furthers such equa- nimity and so on, then it is considered healthy, or wholesome. The result is what amounts to a very ancient diagnostic and statistical manual, if you will: a model of the mind that analyzes different states of mind and categorizes them as healthy or unhealthy.

Many states of mind that are considered perfectly normal in Western psychology are seen as pathology in this Buddhist psychology. The unwholesome set are what are called the afflictive emotions, or afflictive mental factors; 'emotions' is not quite the right term because some of these properties are cognitive, or perceptual, while others are what we would recognize as emotion. A cursory description of some key unwholesome mental factors will give you the flavor of this system.

The primary unhealthy mental factor is *delusion,* or ignorance, a perceptual element defined as a cloudiness of mind that leads to misperception, confusion and bewilderment. Delusion keeps us from seeing things clearly. It is the fundamental root of suffering—the simple failure to see things without bias of any kind. From a Western psychological point of view we would say that it is defended perception, as opposed to perception that does not need to hide anything from itself, which has no fear.

The second unhealthy factor is attachment, a somewhat archaic term. I think a better, more current term may be *clinging*, because the flavor of it is a selfish longing to satisfy desire, which exaggerates the attractiveness of that which is desired. It is a desire that distorts. It speaks to an addictive quality of longing. In this model, attachment is selfish, love is not.

The third is anger, hostility, or *ill will*, an intense aversion that distorts reality, too, but in the opposite direction from clinging. It makes us see things in a disagreeable light. It bewilders, deludes and disturbs the mind.

The fourth is self-importance, or *conceit*, an inflated or superior self-image that makes us, to quote one source, 'envious of superiors, competitive with equals and arrogant toward inferiors.' Now the Abhidharma model is an extremely thorough catalogue of mind, so I will not go into the seven varieties of conceit that have been described.

Another unwholesome factor is '*wrong*' or 'afflicted' *views*, that is to say the misapprehension or misdiscernment of things. Having misperceived because of ignorance, you continue to misconstrue. I would like to point out, too, that all these factors can be mapped easily in terms of cognitive science. We are talking about a fundamental, perceptual distortion that then, in the flow of information, leads to miscategorizations, and to emotional reactions tied to those miscategorizations.

Another key afflictive factor is indecisiveness, or *perplexity*, the inability to decide. The mind is filled with extreme doubt; you are so bewildered that you are paralyzed with indecision.

There are several derivative afflictions where these factors mix together. From anger, for instance, come wrath, vengeance, spite and envy, and from attachment such things as avarice, smugness, excitement and agitation. Excitement in Abhidharma psychology is understood to characterize the mind of normal people very often because, to quote the same source, 'it causes the mind to engage in uncontrolled fantasy or frivolity.' That is to say that the stream of awareness as we tend to prefer it is one of excitement and agitation in our normal, natural state—which is different from the 'natural state' in the sense that His Holiness would talk about it.

Excitement is interesting, because from a Western point of view it is not abnormal or pathological. But it becomes so when you try to meditate. Remember, that was one of the key decision rules for whether a mental factor is healthy or unhealthy. If you are too excited, too distracted by fantasy and so on, you simply cannot focus the mind.

There are long lists of afflictive factors. Three that will be familiar to anyone who ever studied the Baltimore Catechism are: envy, sloth and torpor. I think it is no accident that there is a commonality, that you can see parts of the Abhidharma analysis of mind in other religious systems, like Catholicism. I think the perennial philosophy that underlies all religions shows they are seeking the same goal and have very similar insights into what the problem with the human condition really is.

In Buddhism the solution is seen in terms of the healthy, or wholesome, mental factors, which are the antidotes to the unhealthy ones. The first is clarity, or certitude. It is seeing things very clearly, a sharpness of mind that is antithetical to delusion.

Detachment, as it is often translated, is a non-grasping, non-clinging quality of mind. Unfortunately 'detachment' is a rather loaded term in English describing icy coldness—a sort of schizoid attitude that Abhidharma would view as a subtle form of anger. What is meant by detachment in Abhidharma is an attitude that lets go easily and does not cling.

A third wholesome factor is what might be translated as loving kindness. It is antithetical to hatred, to aversion. These three healthy factors oppose what are seen as the three roots of mental suffering: attachment, hatred and delusion.

There are other healthy, wholesome factors. To quickly run down the list, these include: enthusiasm, or energy; faith (or confidence—it is an intelligent faith, a questioning faith, not a blind faith); self-respect; considerateness; conscientiousness; non-violence, or compassion (wishing everyone to be free of suffering is really the sense of it); and equanimity.

So what you get is an operational definition of mental health that says simply that the healthiest person is the person in whose mind none of the unhealthy, unwholesome factors ever arise. That is the ideal type, the prototype of mental health. The problem is, of course, that most of us, most of the time are in states where there is some mix of these things. By these standards we fit Buddha's diagnosis that, 'All worldlings are deranged.' So the question is, what to do?

Now the Abhidharma psychologist realized that simply knowing that a state is unhealthy does little or nothing to end it. If you resent your indecisiveness and wish it would go away, what you are doing is adding aversion and desire to the mix of mental states—you see the difficulty? So the strategy is a sort of aikido approach, where you neither seek healthy states directly nor try to push them away. What you do is meditate.

I am oversimplifying, of course. But, in short, what you do is embark on an entire path of self-discipline, which involves ethical standards and a teacher who really knows what is going on and can help you through pitfalls. But the primary, fundamental psycho-technology is meditation in its many, many varieties. To reframe this, meditation, in terms of cognitive science, is simply the sustained effort to retrain attentional, perceptual habits. The effort is to transform the *process* of consciousness, not its content, and this is where the two paths, East and West, start to diverge.

Now there are a vast array of techniques in Tibetan Buddhism, more than in any other system that I know of. Herbert Benson has told us about the benefits of one of them, the path of one-pointedness as it is seen embodied in the relaxation response, where you bring your mind back to a central point of focus and get the calming effects of that approach. Another is mindfulness, which is really meditation as 'metacognition', in the sense that it is used in cognitive psychology, knowing your own mind. In mindfulness, one tries to develop an

observing awareness within the stream of consciousness, which simply notes what is present in that flow from moment to moment. If
you pursue these paths, either of them, quite diligently, you get to a
point where there are abrupt shifts in perception, meditation-induced
shifts in consciousness. If you pursue one-pointedness—that is, concentration—your contract with yourself is that whenever your mind
wanders you bring it back to the central point of focus. If you are very
good you finally reach a point where all distractions cease; this is an
altered state of consciousness called 'samadhi'.

Some meditation paths use first a one-pointedness method to
strengthen concentration and then shift into a mindfulness approach,
where you watch the flow of mind with a centered awareness that
does not get swept away, but simply notes what arises. With dili-
gence, something quite startling happens: the illusion of the co-
herence of self begins to break down. And that begins another kind of
profound psychological shift, the perception of emptiness.

Meditative paths can be quite complex, as Robert Thurman
showed in describing *gTum-mo*; they are very elegant and very
powerful in their effects. In the West we tend to be naive about how
these things work—we think that if you just get a mantra and sit
down twenty minutes a day, great things are going to happen.
Certain good things *will* happen; Herbert Benson has shown that
with the relaxation response. But these profound changes take a
sustained effort. It is not unusual for a Tibetan 'inner scientist' to go
on retreat for three years, three months and three days and really
work at this, day after day after day, to master one meditation
method, and then another and another. It really takes an intense
effort. When these profound shifts are described, it is as a result of a
sustained effort; we should not think that these shifts are easy to
attain.

It is said that in some areas of Tibet one person in five was a monk
or nun. Now there is an interesting question: Why would a culture
support a class of people who, from a Western point of view, contrib-
uted nothing to the economy? Their job was to cultivate these inner
states. The reason why we even raise the question has to do with a
naive understanding in the West about what is important; it is
because we have a lavish material economy to which—to put it in
psychoanalytical terms—we are extremely overcathected. We expect
too much from it and put too much into it. At the same time, our

inner economy is impoverished by comparison. This is the point that Robert Thurman was making.

Consider the difference between a toxic and a nourishing encounter. You go into a store and buy something, and the sales clerk says, 'Thank you so much,' in a warm, sincere tone. You go into another store, buy something, and the sales clerk says, 'Thank you so much,' in a cold, abrupt tone. The internal state of the person that you deal with—that is, the mental factors that are dominant in the mind of a person at any one moment—define the quality of a certain coin that we exchange in a psychological economy. It is an economy that is doing very poorly; we have too many toxic encounters. Cultures like those of classical India and Tibet understood well the importance of nourishing encounters and the value of having people whose job within that society was to make themselves as nourishing as possible and to teach other people how to do that too. This is something we in the West have not yet understood.

Consider the prototype of a person who, in Tibetan psychology, would be called a *bodhisattva*. This is a main model of mental well-being in Tibetan Buddhism. The chief qualities of such a person are:[30] generosity; self-discipline; patience (which in English is too thin a term—it has the sense of strength and fortitude); energy, or enthusiasm, even for very tough challenges; stability of mind, clear focus; and wisdom, insight into the nature and cause of suffering. All of which allow a person to be skillful in serving others—that is, not looking at a situation in terms of, 'What's in it for me?' but, 'What can I do for you?' And being very good at seeing what that might be, and doing it without even asking the question.

In the Tibetan tradition, the word for 'practice' is the same as that for 'attain'. That is, in a sense, to practice *is* to attain. This is not necessarily just a rarified goal; it is something everyone can cultivate to the extent that they try. His Holiness once gave a list of the signs of the bodhisattva: self-confidence without conceit or pride; determination without craving; caution without discouragement; compassion without attachment—that is, a love that wants nothing in return.

Now I have to shift gears here and adopt a skeptical Western stance because, after all, is such an ideal really possible? It just seems too good to be true, from the Western model of mental health. It questions what we assume to be 'givens' of human nature. The bodhisattva is, from a Western point of view, virtuous beyond belief.

And I think that is why the model is so important—because it challenges our own paradigm. Can there be the complete eradication of unwholesome mental factors from the mind? I surely never read about it in *Archives of General Psychiatry*. But in the classical literature of all great religions that is the prototype, that is the model of mental health. It is a radical transformation that overreaches the goals of Western therapies. It is the prototype of the saint—a prototype that is notable by its absence not just in Western psychology but in Western systems of thought generally. It is something that we have left behind in recent centuries.

Now, that is not to say that there are not points of convergence between Western and Tibetan psychologies. I think there are many. And there are also many near misses that have to do with how paradigms interact when they contact each other. At the beginning of a dialogue there is often great resistance. I think that was true around the turn of the century. William James, though not a resister, said something telling:

> The faculty of voluntarily bringing back a wandering attention over and over again is the very root of judgment, character and will. An education which should improve this faculty would be the education *par excellence*. But it is easier to define this ideal than to give practical directions for bringing it about.[31]

Bringing the wandering attention back over and over again is the fundamental instruction in meditation, of course.

James had no access to that; he studied religion but I do not think he knew much about the technologies of religion, the inner psychologies. In the chapter on attention in his classic textbook on psychology of 1910, he said that he had tried to keep his mind on one thing for more than a few moments and found it impossible. And that has been the assumption in Western cognitive science ever since. We really have relegated attention to a restricted kind of study. We never consider how far we might push the ability to voluntarily attend and what the benefits might be. What if James had studied *gTum-mo*? Where would psychology be today? Where would cognitive science be today!

Jung had an odd relationship with Eastern religions because he was very taken by the notion of the mandala and the power of the mandala, but he put down people from the West who tried to study Eastern techniques. He said:

> People will do anything, no matter how absurd, in order to avoid facing their own souls. They will practice yoga and all its exercises, observe a strict regimen of diet, learn theosophy by heart, or mechanically repeat mystic texts from the literature of the whole world, all because they cannot get on with themselves and have not the slightest faith that anything useful could ever come out of their own souls.[32]

He was advocating his own variety of depth psychology, of course. But he was rejecting a series of techniques whose benefits he did not really explore.

Freud rejected it all out of hand. In his introduction to *Civilization and Its Discontents*, he refers to a letter he had received from Romaine Rolland (a Nobel laureate and poet who at the time was studying with the Hindu saint Sri Ramakrishna in Calcutta) in which Rolland wrote, I admire your psychological writing and I wonder what you make of this: I sometimes feel something 'limitless and unbounded'. Rolland suggested that this feeling might be the physiological basis of much of mysticism. But Freud says: I have looked everywhere within myself and have failed to find anything like this. It seems to be what we might call an 'oceanic feeling', which is a sign of regression to an infantile state. And it may be the source of religious feeling, but what does that tell you about religion? That is where Freud came out.

William James had a different view; he did not simply dismiss things out of hand. He said of the state of mind that regards Eastern psychologies in this dismissive way:

> We are surely all familiar in a general way with this method of discrediting states of mind for which we have an antipathy. 'Medical materialism' seems indeed a good appellation for the too simple-minded system of thought which we are considering. Medical materialism finishes up St. Paul by calling his vision on the road to Damascus a discharging lesion of the occipital cortex, he being an epileptic. It snuffs out St. Theresa as an hysteric and St. Francis of Assisi as an hereditary degenerate.[33]

I remember when I came back from India and was designing my research on meditation. The whole idea was rather novel at Harvard and I was explaining what a mantra is to one of my clinical psychology professors. I said, you repeat this sound silently over and over and over. And he said, how is that any different from an obsessive patient who keeps repeating 'damn, damn, damn, damn, damn'? He could not get it. That attitude has led to a loss for Western psychology. There is a saying in India, 'When a pickpocket meets a saint, all he sees are his pockets,' and I think that in this great dialogue between East and West we have been seeing too many pockets. That, at least, was true of the early contacts. It has shifted of late, and that is where I would like to end, on the synthesis that seems to be emerging.

One of the first Western psychologists to really have a very thoughtful look at Buddhism was Franz Alexander, who was trained in the Berlin Psychoanalytic Institute in the 1930s and had access to excellent German translations of Eastern texts. He later founded the Chicago Psychoanalytic Institute after coming to this country. Alexander wrote an excellent paper looking at how the processes of psychoanalysis also seem to occur to some degree in meditation. Unfortunately, he titled it 'Buddhistic Training as an Artificial Catatonia,' so it has not been widely read.[34]

On the other hand, there are similarities between models of mental health, East and West. Erik Erikson's final stage of maturity in the life-cycle talks about acceptance of one's life circumstances and absence of fear, especially fear of death. Maslow's 'self-actualized' person has clear perception of reality, detachment, not being swayed by flattery or criticism, an equanimity, a compassion. These are points of convergence, and I think there are many more.

But the telling difference is in the methods, the means to mental health that exist in each system. I think this is one place where there can be really fruitful interchange. By and large, psychotherapy focuses on the *content* of consciousness. It does not attempt the more radical transformation posited in the Tibetan Buddhist approach, which focuses on the *process* of consciousness. Buddhism seeks to free the individual from negative states of mind by altering the workings of perception and cognition. For this reason, I think the similarities in mental health between the systems are on the surface. Western methods do not really attempt the changes in the deep structures of cognition and personality that Tibetan Buddhism proposes.

The most current thought—and some of the most sophisticated—on how these approaches fit together and complement each other is Harvard-based. It comes from people who have studied Abhidharma and similar psychologies of Buddhism as well as psychoanalytic thought. One of these thinkers is Jack Engler, co-author of the book, *Transformations of Consciousness*. His view represents an emerging perspective that when you put the two psychologies together, you get a more complete spectrum of human development. You can trace developmental lines that are well established and well studied in Western psychology and then see how they are extended through these other techniques in the psychologies of the East. For instance, those of you who are familiar with object-relations theory will know that ego identity and object-constancy are signs of psychological maturity. Engler points out that from an Eastern point of view these things dissolve as one advances on the path. That is, what we take as normality in the West is, from the Buddhist point of view, an arrested development. In essence the point is, first you have to put your ego together—then you can give it up.

Mark Epstein, who worked with Herbert Benson at one point, is Harvard-trained and now at Cornell. He is describing two of the main currents of thought in modern psychoanalysis, instinctual libido (Freud's classic sexual and aggressive drives), and a newer concept, object libido (which comes from object-relations and self-psychology) that is seeking relations. He suggests that these are transformed through meditative experiences and sublimated in a way that we do not consider yet in Western psychology: as, on the one hand, wisdom, and on the other, compassion.

Daniel Brown, who is also Harvard-based, puts them together very nicely and I will end by reading a passage from his book. He says:

> Freud once said that the most we could hope for from psychoanalysis or psychotherapy was to replace neurotic conflict with everyday unhappiness. The meditative traditions take up where he left off. They provide a method for focusing on everyday unhappiness and finding a way out. The way involves training attention so that you gain voluntary control over perceptual processes and eventually undercut the roots of reactivity in ordinary biased perception. This eliminates a great deal of suffering, since the bases of

that suffering were in those mechanisms and that reactivity. You thus become a master of your own mind and experience.[35]

He says finally, and his conclusion is also mine, though it is quite different from Freud's, that Tibetan Buddhist psychology shows us 'a way for civilization to grow beyond its discontents.'

Dialogue:
Buddhism, Psychology & the Cognitive Sciences

Diana L. Eck, Ph.D
Professor of Comparative Religion & Indian Studies,
Harvard University

Howard E. Gardner, Ph.D
Professor of Education, Harvard University

Daniel Goleman, Ph.D
Contributing Writer, The New York Times

Robert A. F. Thurman, Ph.D
Jey Tsong Khapa Professor of Indo-Tibetan Buddhist Studies,
Columbia University

Dialogue:
Buddhism, Psychology & the Cognitive Sciences

Introduction by Diana Eck

In 1950, Heinrich Zimmer began his book, *Philosophies of India*, with an arresting statement:

> We of the Occident are about to arrive at a crossroads that was reached by the thinkers of India some seven hundred years before Christ.[36]

I think we have now arrived at this crossroads. It is the crossroads between the exploration of the world outside and the exploration of the inner world of the mind. As Westerners, we have gone to great extremes to understand the outer world. We discovered the so-called 'New World' of the Americas; and we kept on discovering 'new worlds' all the way to the West Coast. We have been to the moon. We have examined the outer world of our physiology and we have come to understand the cellular structure of our bodies. But the exploration of the inner world of the mind is one that for Westerners has in some ways only just begun.

In the dialogue between cultures and religions, the dialogue between science and religion is very important. I myself have been very involved in the inter-religious dialogue between Christians, Buddhists and Muslims. In any such dialogue we put our own views at risk and enter into the mutual shaping and changing that Howard Gardner has mentioned. What, then, is the nature of the dialogue between science in general, and the Tibetan tradition of Buddhist thought in particular, a tradition that has so thoroughly investigated the workings of the mind?

I think that many of us would not get very far with the metaphysical language in which the dialogue is cast. We saw something of this in the vast gulf in understanding that opened as we tried to understand 'emptiness', on the one hand, and the masses of neurons in the brain, on the other. Nevertheless, there is a common agenda and method in the fact that both the mind science of the Buddhist tradition and the explorations of the medical researchers are based on traditions of experimentation and a very carefully refined and disciplined practice. Daniel Goleman mentioned some of the dimensions of that practice from the Buddhist standpoint. It is an experimental practice. It is not a form of religiousness that simply says, 'Believe this on faith.' It is an analysis of the universe, and an understanding of the mind that is an invitation to exploration.

The Buddha did not propound the Four Noble Truths as a theory about the universe. He described the world as sorrow, suffering, perhaps anxiety, or even stress, would be a good translation in our own context. There is a cause for that stress, that anxiety. There is a way out of it; and this is the way. This is not a theory about the universe. It is an experimentally verified analysis of how the universe is. And it is offered not as a creed, but as an invitation to 'come and see'. As the Buddha put it, 'Come and see for yourself.' That is the experimental ground for the dialogue in which we are engaged.

I might say, as someone who studies religion, that it is true that the kinds of practices and discoveries Dr. Benson articulated in *The Relaxation Response* have been verified in religious traditions throughout the world. And yet there is something different about this particular dialogue between scientists and Buddhists. It is not by chance that this is a dialogue between Buddhists and Western medical scientists.

What is different is what Dan Goleman referred to as the articulation of 'technique'. In the Christian mystical writing of the Middle Ages, *The Cloud of Unknowing*, there is a description of a higher state of consciousness found in prayer. Of this prayer, the author says:

> If you were to ask me how to begin to pray, I would just have to ask God, from his grace and his mercy, to teach you himself.

There is no articulation of a technique, or at least not a very elaborate one. But technique is precisely what has been described from the yoga tradition on through the mind science tradition in the East. We do not have to ask God to teach us himself. There is a way to begin: sit down, be quiet, watch your mind, bring it to one-pointedness, bring it back when it strays—which it most certainly will within the first ten seconds—over and over again.

It is technique, and it is an experimental technique that over many hundreds of years has been shown to lead to a knowledge of mind. Now here we are faced with a problem of understanding: How do we know what that knowledge is unless we come and see for ourselves? This is the challenge that Buddhist thinkers have extended to Western mind scientists, that knowledge is based on a willingness to enter into the experiment, to sit down, pick a mantra or word to recite and see what happens.

Panel Discussion

ECK: Professor Thurman, I would like to ask you about the compassion the Dalai Lama emphasized earlier. The techniques of the Tibetan monks' mind discipline are not practiced simply to overcome illness, reduce blood pressure, or relieve the stress of daily life. Their real purpose is to develop compassion. Could you tell us how this practice leads to our becoming more compassionate. Is there a logical link between this kind of knowledge and compassion?

THURMAN: His Holiness mentioned that the notion of karma, or intentional action, did not cover all types of phenomena in the world and gave an example of one that it did not cover: the natural sentient, or animal, desire to be happy. He indicated that this was in the nature of things, that it was a natural law for human beings to desire happiness. I was interested to hear this because it is an unusual formulation in relation to the theory of karma.

The usual formulation is that human beings have become human through a process of evolution—not only as a species but also as individuals—by developing intelligence, diminishing aggressiveness, and becoming more gentle, generous and detached. Even human physiology embodies a tremendous amount of virtue and, in the Buddhist view, the human body evolved from generosity, tolerance and virtue. The myth of the hunter and the aggressive human is not at all the Buddhist view.

His Holiness often talks about the nature of life as being affectionate, referring especially to animals and their young. Mammals, for example, carry babies in their womb, the one being carrying the other inside its own body, nourishing it with its blood stream, giving birth to it in intimate ways, nursing it and so forth. All these elements relate to the fundamental sentient nature of affection, and His Holiness often builds his teachings on compassion around this, side-stepping the evolutionary nature and also the idea that the cultivation of compassion is a specifically religious matter. He often says that compassion is not a matter of religion or of Buddhism, but something essential to every human society.

When he received the Nobel Peace Prize in Oslo two years ago, His Holiness spoke at length about the bees. He explained how the bees have a natural connection to each other, how they function very cooperatively without a police force, without laws and without religions, making honey, which he, the Dalai Lama, likes to snitch! He was very, very amusing.

But this is the first time that I have heard His Holiness elevate the common desire for happiness to a natural law. It is quite striking. It is definitely something new in my own thinking. The way I understand this is that he is connecting it to the basic idea of the clear light mind. The reason why the Buddha declared his teaching as a sort of Good News to the planet was not because he had discovered the First Noble Truth, that everything is suffering. In fact he did not even mean that *every*thing is suffering—he meant that every *unenlightened-and-selfishness-dominated*-thing is suffering. His real truth, the one that Buddhists actually take refuge in, was the Third Noble Truth, the truth of freedom from all suffering; of freedom as the reality of life, that beings are free, and that they therefore have the right to happiness, naturally. This is why the Buddha was so cheerful.

The cultivation of compassion is possible because it is based on reality. If evil were the more powerful reality, then the cultivation of compassion would be a pipe-dream. But since the deeper nature of reality is freedom and love, the way to cultivate compassion is through wisdom. In other words, the reason we are not compassionate in a reality where we have abundance, where we have sensitivity, where we have each other, where we have interconnection with a miraculous web of beauty, generosity and so on, is that our ignorance makes us try to grab things for ourselves. Our basic ignorance makes us reject other people and fight—us against this vast thing—and think that we are somehow separate, which we are not. There is no separate thing, no independent, absolutely-established 'I' unconnected to the rest of the universe. Since this ignorance is based on an illusion, it is weaker than the wisdom that sees that we are interconnected with everything. When we know this, others' feelings become our feelings, their wish for happiness becomes ours, and all this connectedness becomes mutually positive.

ECK: Professor Gardner, you suggested that this kind of dialogue introduces the risk of our having to change our minds about some things. Has the interaction in this symposium led you to question anything in your own way of thinking?

GARDNER: I was pretty much a blank slate on the topic of Buddhism before I came. One of the things that as a result of my science I believe very strongly is that cognitively we are a set of what I would call schemata, theories and expectations. Some of these may be preordained by species membership, the Kantian kind of things I mentioned before. It is very hard to think about the world except in terms of objects, space, time and so on, but even at the age of four or five, humans develop extremely powerful theories about how the world works, how their mind works, how other minds work and what life is about. Education often does not impact these because they are so fundamentally built into ourselves.

Now there have been two challenges to that belief system, which I think is fairly strongly held by people who are into the cognitive domain and believe that you cannot see the world fresh but are a victim of your theories, concepts and stereotypes. One is the notion that you could get clear, wipe out, at least temporarily, these ideas and notions and look at the world emptily, or in a clear light state. The other is the notion that you can devote many years to the cultivation of a better understanding of yourself and your con- sciousness, and for other people to appreciate that, as Robert Thur- man just said, they have to do the same kind of thing. These are both things that I really do not understand. But if either of them is true, it shakes up the way I think about things.

ECK: Daniel Goleman said that part of our problem as human beings is that we cannot pay attention, we cannot keep our mind on one thing in a disciplined way for very long unless we practice. Does that agree with what you know about mind?

GARDNER: I guess I would agree, although I would not want to get into the technical issue of millisecond to millisecond. But I would not agree with the implication that it is an unnatural thing to do. Cultures make it natural or unnatural. One of the reasons why I am very interested in China in particular is because from an early age, both at home and in the educational system, there is a cultivation of practices and skills over a long period of time. So flitting around is as unnatural in some Oriental contexts as is sticking to something for a long time in ours.

I often point out to educators that both the very underprivileged and the very overprivileged in our society suffer from the same thing: the lack of inclination to attend closely to something for long periods of time. The underprivileged do not have the opportunity, the over-privileged have so many possibilities that they flit from one thing to another. I do not think it is a question of being natural or unnatural, but rather of cultural expectations. Certainly infants can stare at mobiles for an awfully long time . . .

GOLEMAN: There is a distinction that needs to be made here, and this is what James was getting at. James was not questioning the ability to focus on something for a sustained period. We can all do that, particularly on things in which we are interested, though Asian cultures are generally better than Western ones at training children to do so. He was talking about the ability to sustain attention *without distraction*. That is what he said he could not do, and that is what Buddhism teaches.

GARDNER: Was it his response to a stream of consciousness in which new things keep coming up?

GOLEMAN: Exactly, and the Tibetans are talking about a focused stream of consciousness that is completely sustained. This is a quantum leap from the Chinese example.

ECK: As someone who has gone deeply into the study of forms of meditation, would you comment on the earlier presentation of the relaxation response by Herbert Benson? He likened this to a door that opens onto other territory. What has your study of meditation told you about where we go once have walked through the door?

GOLEMAN: Where one ends up depends on what one does. As Herbert Benson pointed out, the relaxation response is the most generic effect of one-pointedness training of attention, of that kind of meditation, but there are many different techniques. There are prob-ably more schools of meditation and specific techniques in Tibetan

Buddhism than there are schools of therapy in Western psychotherapy—which is to say, a lot—and each one represents a different method of training awareness. So where you end up depends on where you start out and what you do.

However, what you get is an empirical question and the empiricism that needs to evolve is one that combines Western methodologies and Eastern inner science, so that we have a more sophisticated and precise way of asking those questions.

ECK: Do people come to a certain form of Tibetan Buddhism because of who their spiritual master is, or is it more that they feel their own way and happen to end up in one stream rather than another?

THURMAN: It varies. Many people come to a particular teacher and follow his way, although a good teacher will not teach a single way to all students. There will be those for whom the teacher will emphasize, for instance, some sort of faith or refuge practice, an emotional unlocking; for others he will recommend some strongly intellectual path; and there will be those for whom he emphasizes a strong meditation practice.

One of my early teachers, for example, used to take great delight in preventing me from meditating. When I was a monk in his monastery, if he caught me meditating he would chase me out to plant flowers or do things like that. At the same time, I was learning a lot and he was making me re-examine and re-evaluate things, but he would never let me get into quietistic states because he said that these could become addictive and I would get into thinking that this was the only thing to do and become uninvolved with the world, spending all my time in retreat. I would sneak out and hide in the outhouse, where I would sit meditating, and at that very moment he would show up and stop me!

Certain teachers will say that this or that is the only thing to do, but the good ones realize that people are incredibly varied and need different methods.

Questions from the Audience

AUDIENCE: Many Westerners turn to Eastern spiritual teachers hoping to find in them the same ideals that you have described. Can you comment on this in view of the fact that a number of students have been disappointed in the last couple of decades by the alleged peccadilloes of teachers in various traditions?

GOLEMAN: One of the catch-22s of this field is trying to develop an objective verification of someone's internal status. This is a very Western thing to want to do: Is he really an arhat? Is he really a bodhisattva? An additional problem and paradox is that this ideal type of enlightened being cultivates humility. Westerners have often been attracted to people who advertise. My experience is that these two things do not go together. Disappointments have come from people from whom it perhaps ought not to have come as a surprise, especially given the idealizing transference that people bring to this kind of relationship and the temptations of countertransference. It is a set-up for an explosion, and that is what we have often seen. So the methodological problem is that it is extremely hard to verify what attainments somebody has.

AUDIENCE: I would like to question what you said about the concept that Western psychoanalysis, or psychotherapy, changes the content rather than the structure of consciousness. It seems to me that the free associative process encouraged in analysis is a lot like mindfulness meditation—observing ego much like the development of an observing consciousness. I wonder if we could wind up being more optimistic about Freud's techniques than he was himself?

GOLEMAN: It is interesting. The stance that Freud suggested for therapists, for the analyst, in his famous lecture on lay analysis was an 'even-hovering attention'. An even-hovering attention sounds very much like mindfulness. So I would say that within psychoanalysis the closest approximation to an Eastern technique of mindfulness is the stance of the therapist. Free association is a beginning, but, from the point of view of mindfulness, it is rather sloppy. It serves a certain purpose but it does not make the individual more precise about the moment to moment categories of mind that arise. So from a technical point of view it differs, but I would say that generally it is a good beginning.

AUDIENCE: I am curious about what I see as a fundamental tension between the Buddhist approach to mental health and the mind and the psychoanalytic approach, with respect to the role of aggression or the parts of the self that are described as aggressive and sadistic. In the psychoanalytic approach you have to own, acknowledge and integrate those parts of yourself into your nature. The Buddhist approach seems to attempt to transcend it, to come to a place where these do not exist as a part of the self. What I worry about is the attempt to reach this state where aggression and sadism are transcended without having worked through them. Clinically, what I have seen sometimes in those who are very involved in Buddhist practice is a warding off of the aggressive and sadistic aspects of the self, which then get acted out in all kinds of ways. In Buddhism, do you need to work through the aggression before you can transcend it, or can you just bypass it altogether?

THURMAN: Buddhism can be seen as simply wanting to ward off anger and aggression. And Buddhism does teach that hatred—hatred, I think, is the clearest way to translate it—is a very negative energy that poisons the person who holds it and leads him or her to act in ways that cause harm to those towards whom it is directed. However, interestingly, sometimes the antidote, or one of the preventative measures against feeling hatred, is to be aggressive, in the sense of outwardly energetic in preventing a very negative situation arising that would cause you to feel hatred, for example.

Similarly, when the energy that is normally tied up in cycles of hatred is finally transmuted—not transcended but transmuted—through a new kind of understanding of the situation, it becomes the very energy of *gTum-mo*, psychic heat. *gTum-mo* is called 'furor meditation', and furor means something like the fury that a warrior feels. But this furor is completely dis-identified from the hatred that says, 'I want to go get some person,' and turned into, 'I want to clear away ignorance from the world.' So the issue of integration and transcendence is much too complicated to answer briefly, but I think that common ground can be found between Buddhism and the psychological disciplines on this point. I also think Buddhism has a lot to contribute.

GOLEMAN: The question whether, from the Buddhist point of view, aggression or any of the other negative mental factors could become a problem along the way is probably best addressed by Jack Engler in *Transformations of Consciousness*, where he talks about higher pathologies. My own understanding is that, at least for many of us in the West, a spiritual practice is well complemented by a good psycho-therapy. The two are not oppositional at all but can work together very well.

AUDIENCE: You spoke previously about a definition of maturity according to Tibetan psychology that involves compassion and the fusion of the self, getting beyond the ego. This reminded me of some readings I have seen by people like Carol Ann Gilligan and other women psychologists. What similarities do you see between Tibetan psychology and some of the psychologies presented by American women?

GOLEMAN: If you map out the systems, then since both Buddhism and Carol Gilligan's and like thought posit a moral ethic based on relationship, there are probably many, many overlaps. I think that this is one of the great points of contact between the psychologies of East and West.

Conclusion

Looking Ahead

The dialogue between the psychologies of Buddhism and the West represents the meeting of disparate paradigms, each with its own special lens on the human experience. It is in just such an intellectual encounter that an entirely new synthesis can evolve.

As these systems, so separate for so long, continue their encounter, there is a rich opportunity for cross-fertilization. Cognitive science, for instance, may find a wealth of insights and hypotheses about extending the limits of attention; contemporary models of mental health and of personality may find a challenge to what they had assumed were the limits of human potential.

And just as there may be much that modern psychology can learn from an ancient inner science, there may, in turn, be ways that Abhidharma and other Eastern systems of thought can benefit from what modern science has discovered about the mind and the brain. Indeed, as His Holiness has said about the dialogue between Buddhism and science, if modern science has proven some Buddhist belief to be wrong, then Buddhism will have to change. I trust that, in this meeting of the ways, modern psychology will be as flexible.

This symposium is one of several that have taken place by now between His Holiness and modern scientists. His Holiness has set the example of representing Tibetan Buddhist thought with great integrity, while remaining open to whatever truths have emerged from the efforts of modern science.

The dialogue could benefit by including a wider range of representatives from the Tibetan side, so that His Holiness—who is ever more pressed for time in his role as world statesman and leader of the Tibetan people—does not have to carry the dialogue alone. If other Tibetan scholars are included and the dialogue carried on in a more sustained way—over months and years rather than a day or two—there could a more systematic and fruitful intellectual yield.

New institutions may be required to expand the Western research universities and the Tibetan monastic universities that presently nurture and develop Western researchers and Eastern mind scientists. The Tibetan monastic university needs facilities that can expand the traditional training to include skills that will enhance the ability to dialogue with modern scientists. And the Western research university needs institutes for advanced study of mind sciences that can enhance the researcher's ability to dialogue with Tibetan inner scientists. Each institution needs the long-term presence of visiting researchers from the other, so that there can be long-term working contact between the traditions.

Through such an intellectual partnership the rich insights and methods of the Tibetan inner sciences could be explored more systematically. Modern psychologists, working in partnership with Tibetan experts, might then, for instance, plan a program of research that could investigate avenues such as the cognitive, perceptual and neurophysiological correlates of attentional training. Similar partnerships might fruitfully explore, for instance, the mind/body interface—as Herbert Benson's initial studies of *gTum-mo* show, the Tibetan inner sciences have reached understandings of the mind's capacity for affecting the body that exceed anything known yet in the West.

The net result of such a systematic, sustained mutual exploration would certainly be to extend our understanding of the human condition in ways that could have wide practical benefits. And that, after all, is a goal shared by both the ancient inner sciences and their modern counterparts.

DANIEL GOLEMAN
ROBERT A. F. THURMAN

Contributors

Speakers

HIS HOLINESS THE FOURTEENTH DALAI LAMA, the spiritual and temporal leader of Tibet, is internationally recognized as a spokesman for peace, nonviolence and understanding among different cultures and religions. He has resided in exile in India since 1959, when China forcefully occupied Tibet. He heads the Tibetan government in exile in Dharamsala, India, and has worked to establish educational, cultural and religious institutions to preserve the Tibetan culture. In 1989, he received the Nobel Peace Prize for his efforts to find a peaceful solution to the Tibetan struggle for liberty.

HERBERT BENSON, MD, is Associate Professor of Medicine at the Harvard Medical School, Chief of the Division of Behavioral Medicine at the New England Deaconess Hospital and President of the Mind/Body Medical Institute, Boston. Dr. Benson is a pioneer in the field of behavioral medicine, having devoted more than twenty-five years to researching the mind's impact on the body's health. His research led to the first published description of the relaxation response, an innate physiologic response that counteracts the harmful effects of stress, described in his best-selling book, *The Relaxation Response*. He is a Fellow of the American College of Cardiology and the Society of Behavioral Medicine.

ROBERT A. F. THURMAN, PH.D, is Jey Tsong Khapa Professor of Indo-Tibetan Buddhist Studies at Columbia University, New York. Widely recognized as a Buddhist studies scholar and writer, and highly acclaimed as one of the foremost lecturers on Tibetan Buddhism. His initial interest in Eastern religion and culture was enhanced by living several years as a monk in a Tibetan Buddhist monastery. As President of the American Institute for Buddhist Studies, he convened the First Inner Science Conference with His Holiness the Dalai Lama at Amherst College in 1984. He is also a founding trustee of Tibet House New York.

HOWARD E. GARDNER, PH.D, is a research psychologist who investigates human cognitive capacities, particularly those central to the arts, in normal children, gifted children and brain-damaged children. He currently serves as Professor of Education and Co-Director of Project Zero at the

Harvard Graduate School of Education, Research Psychologist at the Boston Veterans Administration Medical Center, and Adjunct Professor of Neurology at the Boston University School of Medicine. He is the author of over 250 articles in professional journals and periodicals and of ten books.

DANIEL GOLEMAN, PH.D, is a psychologist and award-winning journalist, who reports on behavioral sciences for the *New York Times*. His areas of research and commentary include Asian psychological systems and relaxation techniques, meditation and stress. He is a member of the Scientific Advisory Board of the Mind/Body Medical Institute and a Tibet House New York committee member. He is also a founding member of the Mind and Life Research Network.

Panelists

DAVID M. BEAR, MD, is Professor of Psychiatry at the University of Massachusetts Medical School, Boston. He is interested in the neurological basis of human emotions, specifically the structures within the human brain that regulate emotions such as anger, fear and sexual desire. During a Harvard University Fellowship, he studied differing perspectives on the mind/body connection in such diverse cultures as Japan, India, Israel and the Soviet Union.

DIANA L. ECK, PH.D, is Professor of Comparative Religion and Indian Studies at Harvard University, and an authority on Indian culture and religion. She lectures world-wide and has received numerous grants and awards for her research and writing on South Asian religious beliefs and practices. Among her activities promoting understanding between different religious groups, she chairs the American Academy of Religion Section on Religion in South Asia and the World Council of Churches Working Group on Dialogue with People of Living Faiths.

THUBTEN JINPA, one of the principal translators to His Holiness the Dalai Lama, studied Buddhist philosophy, epistemology and logic at Shartse College of Ganden University in India, receiving his Geshe degree in 1989. He is presently studying at Kings College, Cambridge University in England.

STEVEN W. MATTHYSSE, PH.D, is Associate Professor of Psychobiology at Harvard Medical School and a psychobiologist at McLean Hospital. He is known nationally for his efforts to apply mathematical models to brain biology and to normal and abnormal psychology. Dr. Matthysse has been very involved in the search for genes that may contribute to mental illness. Recently, he has been developing mathematical equations to describe the continually changing electrical patterns of the nervous system, which he believes provide an important link between the brain and conscious experience.

DAVID D. POTTER, PH.D, is Robert Winthrop Professor of Neurobiology at Harvard University, and known for his work in neurobiology. His research led to the discovery that nerve cells can communicate via electrical as well as chemical signals. He also helped develop a culture medium in which a single nerve cell can be grown—a finding that has prompted researchers to study detailed nerve cell activity. Among his current interests are the biological factors that contribute to addiction and psychosis.

JOSEPH J. SCHILDKRAUT, MD, is Professor of Psychiatry at Harvard Medical School and recognized internationally for his research on biochemical factors in depressive illnesses. His current research focuses on the biochemistry of depression and schizophrenia, and the ways in which antidepressant and antipsychotic drugs interact with the brain. He also studies mood disorders and spirituality in visual artists. Dr. Schildkraut is a member of the Board of Trustees of the Mind/Body Medical Institute and chairman of its Scientific Advisory Board.

CARL E. SCHWARTZ, MD, is an Instructor in Psychiatry at the Harvard Medical School whose research has focused on affective and anxiety disorders in children and adolescents, and the biological correlates of personality. His other interests include psychiatric epidemiology, the philosophy of psychiatry, and the interaction between psychopharmacology and psychotherapy. Recently he received a five-year grant from the National Institute for Mental Health to study the relationships between behavior and physiology in children as they mature.

Notes

Preface

1. Alexandra David-Neel, *Magic and Mystery in Tibet*, Ch. VI.

Chapter One

2. Taking refuge in the three jewels of Buddhism is generally considered the way to become a Buddhist. The words 'I go for refuge to the Buddha, to the Dharma, to the Sangha' are recited daily by Buddhists all over the world. Those who take refuge do so because they recognize the danger of the ignorance-driven world and fear to be reborn again and again in states of woe such as hells, ghost realms and animal kingdoms or as humans in horrible circumstances. They consider that the *Buddha* found a way to freedom from such a fate; taught the *Dharma*, which is that way; and founded the *Sangha*, or community, that follows the way. Taking refuge in these three, which are perceived to be like wish-granting jewels by those in fear of worlds of suffering, is the beginning of the Buddhist path to freedom.

3. The teaching on the Four Noble Truths was the Buddha's first. Like a medical analysis, these truths express his diagnosis and prognosis of all life, and especially the human condition, and provide a methodical therapy for suffering. They are called 'noble' because they are under-stood to be true for a 'noble' person, one who has awoken from the sleep of selfishness. Enumerated, they are the truth of suffering—the inevita-ble experience of the egocentric being; origination—how ignorance, greed and hate combine with evolution to cause that suffering; cessa-tion—how freedom from suffering is possible; and the path—the way to achieve that freedom by counteracting the causes of suffering.

4. Explained below. See also *Opening the Eye of New Awareness*, pp. 39ff.

5. This verse, common in all Buddhist sources, is cited in Shantarakshita's *Compendium of All Principles*, v. 3587.

6. This is the Vijnanavada, or Cittamatra, the Idealistic school of Ma-hayana Buddhist philosophy, elaborated in the fourth-century CE by the great Indian philosophers Asanga and Vasubandhu. Much more sophis-ticated than a mere solipsism, it used mentalistic reductionism to focus a

very penetrating investigation of the mental processes that structure our perceptions of objects, control our reactions and drive our actions. It engaged in vigorous debate over many centuries with other more realistic schools, as well as with the critical relativists of the Madhyamika schools.

7. This is according to the Abhidharmic cosmology commonly used by most Buddhist schools. The original state is seen as being part of a beginningless cycle of emergences and dissolutions of universes, as Buddhist science always considered the concept of a 'first beginning' unjustifiable and irrational in any of the cosmologies in which it was advanced.

8. See Chapter 4, where such methods of manipulating meditative states are compared to software programs for the brain, especially pp. 67–72.

9. See, for example, Chapter 3, pp. 44–5.

Chapter Two

10. Most Buddhist epistemologies list six consciousnesses, the five that pick up the input from the sense organs of sight, hearing, smell, taste and touch, and a sixth, the mental consciousness. The mental consciousness coordinates the data received via the senses and organizes them by comparing them with concepts and memories. It has no corresponding organ, except by analogy, though it does have an object realm—the realm of ideas, images and concepts.

11. The Prasangika (Dialectical) branch of the Madhyamika (Centrist or Middle Way) school is considered in the Tibetan university curriculum to be the most subtle and advanced of all Buddhist philosophical schools. Founded by Buddhapalita in the fourth century CE, it was elaborated by Chandrakirti in the sixth century and implemented most fully for the Tibetan context by Tsong Khapa in the early fifteenth century. It is a school of critical relativism. See Jeffrey Hopkins, *Meditation on Emptiness*; and Robert A. F. Thurman, *The Central Philosophy of Tibet*.

12. I.e. can mathematics can be understood as a kind of convention, or conventional language, and would a scientist parallel the Buddhist's statement that 'things exist only conventionally' with the statement that 'things exist only mathematically'.

Chapter Three

13. See p. 10.

14. The findings described here are published in the scientific journal *Nature* 295 (1982), pp. 234–6.

15. Similar research work is being undertaken by Dr. David Spiegel and his colleagues.

Chapter Four

16. Sanskrit, *adyatmavidya*; Tibetan, *nang-gi rig-pa*.
17. Dharmakirti is renowned as one of the 'Six Ornaments of India', the founding fathers of Indo-Tibetan inner science, and as a world-class philosopher on a par with the best of the European empiricists. For details of his life and a sketch of the early tradition, see Robert Thurman, *The Central Philosophy of Tibet,* Introduction.
18. This gives the best overview to date of the cognitive science movement.
19. Various lists of 'outer' sciences are given in Indian literatures, most commonly breaking them into four: linguistics, logic, medicine (including zoology, botany, chemistry, as well as physiology) and the creative arts (including art, architecture, dance, aesthetics, agriculture, engineering).
20. See pp. 27ff.
21. See p. 24.
22. Ram Dass, *How Can I Help?*, pp. 117–21.
23. I used to love accompanying Dr. Yeshe Donden as he did the rounds in Western hospitals and watching the looks on young and old doctors' faces alike as he dipped the tip of his finger into the patient's urine and tasted it before giving his opinion. This degree of contact with the sick being is beyond our social constraints.
24. A *mani*-wheel is a machine that Tibetans make to generate prayers. It is usually in the form of a cylinder with OM MANI PADME HUM written outside it and upon millions of scrolls packed within it. This is rotated by hand, wind or water to send out prayers for the welfare of all beings. When Tibetans recite OM MANI PADME HUM aloud, they visualize such a wheel slowly revolving in the center of their heart complex, radiating light rays that bless all the beings in the universe. The *gTum-mo* yogi, while not necessarily using OM MANI PADME HUM as the mantra on which he focuses, also visualizes radiating blessed energy as part of his practice.

Chapter Five

25. Howard E. Gardner, *The Mind's New Science.*
26. Richard Rorty, *Philosophy and the Mirror of Nature.*
27. Howard E. Gardner, *The Mind's New Science.*
28. Howard E. Gardner, *Frames of Mind.*

Chapter Six

29. My main source of reference on Tibetan Abhidharma is Geshe Rabten, *The Mind and Its Functions*. I also benefitted from discussions with B. Alan Wallace.

30. One of the best descriptions of the qualities of a bodhisattva is to be found in Shantideva's classic *Guide to the Bodhisattva's Way of Life*.

31. William James, *Principles of Psychology*, p. 424.

32. C. G. Jung, 'Psychology and Alchemy,' *Collected Works*, Vol. 12, pp. 101–2.

33. William James, *The Varieties of Religious Experience*, p. 29.

34. Franz Alexander, *The Scope of Psychoanalysis*.

35. Daniel P. Brown, 'The Transformation of Consciousness in Meditation,' *Noetic Sciences Review* (Spring 1988), p. 16.

Chapter Seven

36. Heinrich Zimmer, *Philosophies of India*, p. 1.

Glossary

Abhidharma. Defined by Vasubandhu as pure wisdom, its correlating mental factors and the clear science that leads to its attainment. Secondarily, it is one of the three collections of canonical Buddhist texts, the other two being Vinaya and Sutra. Abhidharma texts contain a systematic analysis of mind and universe.

Afflictive emotions. The mental mechanisms that cause suffering for beings addicted to them. The six fundamental ones are misknowledge, wrong views, greed, hate, envy and self-righteousness; there are twenty derivative afflictions. Buddhist psychology aims primarily at developing understanding, control of, and eventually freedom from all these afflictions and their instinctual roots.

Arhat. A Buddhist saint who has realized the wisdom of selflessness to a certain degree but is not yet a Buddha, because of his or her lack of the necessary merit and compassion.

Bodhisattva. A messianic hero or heroine who has developed the resolve to free all beings from suffering and has vowed to attain complete enlightenment in order to be able to do so.

Buddha. A perfectly enlightened being, believed not only to have attained omniscience—the direct comprehension of all necessary knowledge in the universe—but also the complete development of universal compassion for all beings, enabling him or her to manifest as whatever is needed for beings to achieve liberation from suffering. Buddhists believe that Buddhahood is the supreme goal of all evolution and that it is eventually attainable by every living being. The historical Buddha, Shakyamuni, lived and taught in India 2,500 years ago. *See* Three jewels.

Clear light mind. The extremely subtle mind of every living being, embodied in what is called the 'indestructible drop', the extremely subtle body. It is this mind that proceeds from life to life, carrying what are called the spiritual genes of the individual continuum. This mind is presented as sort of a subatomic and subcellular mind, of which the tantric yogi/yogini strives to develop direct awareness. Uncovering of this awareness is simultaneous with liberation and enlightenment.

Dependent origination. The fundamental insight of the Buddha, equivalent to emptiness, also translatable as universal relativity. As a theoretical framework for the scientific investigation of individual and cosmic origination, it consists of twelve links, beginning with misknowledge and ending with death. As the philosophical equivalent of emptiness, it signifies the relativity of all things on the levels of causality, psychophysical structure and concept-object relations.

Dharma. Vasubandhu listed eleven main meanings derived from the verb *dhr*, 'to hold'. It can mean a distinct 'phenomenon' that holds a particular character, or the particular 'character' itself. It can also mean 'custom', 'duty', 'law' or 'religion', which hold behavior in patterns. But the essence of the Buddha's discovery was the essential reality of freedom, which can be realized by the human mind as its own deepest condition. The realized individual is then *held apart* from suffering, *held out* of any binding pattern. This gave a new range of meanings to Dharma: the 'Teaching', the 'Path' of practice of the teaching, and the 'Freedom' of that reality, or truth, nirvana itself.

Enlightenment. Any state of increased intelligence, awareness or wisdom. Its main forms are those of the arhat, who has direct understanding of the nature of the self, and of the Buddha, who has complete understanding of all aspects of reality accompanied by universal compassion for all beings. *See also* Buddha.

Four Noble Truths. Called 'noble' because they are understood to be true for a 'noble' person, they are the truths of suffering—the inevitable experience of the egocentric being; origination of suffering—how ignorance, greed and hatred combine with evolution to cause that suffering; cessation of suffering—the reality of freedom from suffering; and the path to the cessation of suffering—the way to achieve that freedom by overcoming the causes of suffering.

Karma. Derived from Sanskrit *kr*, 'to do' or 'to make', karma means intentional action that impacts on the actor's development. Originally in the Vedic culture it meant 'ritual action', since a being's destiny was believed to be controlled by the gods and to be affected by ritual propitiation of the gods. The Buddha redefined karma as physical, verbal and mental ethical action, fitting with his teaching that one's fate is controlled by one's acts and understandings. It is very close to what modern people mean by evolutionary action, except that the feedback mutations from habitual actions are carried by the individual from life to life instead of by a species, and they are not merely random.

Mahayana. The universal or messianic vehicle of Buddhism, believed by Tibetans to have come from Shakyamuni Buddha's teaching but only to have emerged into prominence in India and around Asia four hundred years after his passing away. It adds to the liberational impulse in the individual or monastic vehicle of early Buddhism, the social teaching of universal love and compassion, teaching the goal of liberating and transforming the entire universe of beings, not just the individual.

Mandala. Originally referring to a magic circle of protection, it came to mean an entirely purified environment, such as those in which the many Buddhas make their divine homes. Imaginations of mandalic realms are used in tantric visualization to develop in the meditator a sense of perfect peace, security and joyfulness.

Mantra. A formulaic syllable, word or phrase used to generate a state of awareness, embodiment or manifestation of wisdom or compassion either to intensify the practitioner's own enlightenment or to share that enlightenment with others.

Meditation. A general term for the methodical utilization of attention, thought or concentration to realize specific understandings or insights. Its two main varieties are focused and analytic, each of which has literally innumerable subvarieties. The three steps essential in the process of understanding something deeply or of gaining wisdom are learning, critical reflection and concentrated meditation.

Neurobiology. The science of life as applied especially to the brain, in the attempt to understand mental and emotional states as produced by brain states and functions.

Neuronet model. A model of brain function and cognition related to the so-called holographic paradigm, wherein information is processed multidimensionally in the synaptic neural network of the brain.

OM MANI PADME HUM. The basic mantra of Avalokitesvara, the celestial bodhisattva of great compassion, of whom His Holiness the Dalai Lama is believed to be an incarnation. *OM* is the mantric syllable of embodiment, the invocation of the universal and divine. *Mani* literally means a jewel, referring symbolically to the universal compassion of all Buddhas. *Padma* means lotus, a symbol of the wisdom of selflessness. *HUM* is the mantric syllable of mind, representing the integration of the universal within the individual. Therefore, the repetition of the mantra as a whole conjures a sense of well-being from affirming the omnipresence of the union of wisdom and compassion, the fact for faith that wisdom/compassion is the strongest force in the universe and triumphs over all apparent evils and sufferings.

Path. A term widely used in Buddhism to signify a process of development and transformation.

Prasangika. The Prasangika (Dialectical) branch of the Madhyamika (Centrist, or Middle Way) school is considered in the Tibetan university curriculum to be the most subtle and advanced of all Buddhist philosophical schools. It was founded by Buddhapalita in the fourth century CE, elaborated by Chandrakirti in the sixth century and implemented most fully for the Tibetan context by Tsong Khapa in the early fifteenth century. It is a school of critical relativism, extremely relevant to the debate on relativism current in modern philosophical circles.

Radical materialism. The metaphysical view that matter/energy is the only reality in the universe, believing that reductionistic, or phsyicalistic, explanations are the only ones with any vitality or usefulness. It specifically excludes consideration of mind as having any physical reality that must be taken into account in scientific investigations.

Reality. The status of something as being there in the way it appears to be. In Buddhism there are considered to be two realities, ultimate and relative, which are key in the practice of Buddhist philosophy and science.

Refuge. See Three jewels.

Samadhi. One of the main terms for meditation, referring especially to a type of balanced concentration that can generate transformed states of awareness, or even, in advanced practitioners, transformations of reality.

Samsara. A term used for the unenlightened life of humans and other types of being, implying an endless round of sufferings caused by living in the impossible situation of feeling oneself a separate individual up against an infinite and eternal universe.

Sangha. The Buddhist community, one of the three jewels of refuge.

Sentient being. A being with individual sensibility living as a beginningless and endless continuum, suffering as long as unenlightened about the egocentric addiction pattern, happy once so enlightened.

Sutra. The term used for a canonical Buddhist text that purports to record the actual sayings of the Buddha.

Tantra. A technology for spiritual realization used by both Buddhists and Hindus. The Buddhist tantras were developed in rich profusion in ancient India and are preserved in the main only in Tibetan civilization.

Theravada. The Pali word for Sthaviravada, eight of the eighteen schools of early Buddhism. The Theravadins missionarized Sri Lanka during the time of Ashoka in the third century BCE and their form of Buddhism survived there and eventually spread to Burma, Thailand and Cambodia. Primarily a monastic Buddhism, it has tended to coexist uneasily with Mahayana Buddhism in most countries. However, in Tibet, the land of monasteries, where over 6,000 of the largest monasteries in the world existed until the Chinese invasion of the 1950s, monastic Buddhism and messianic Buddhism coexisted in close contact, just as they had for 1,500 years in India.

Three jewels. Taking refuge in the three jewels of Buddhism is generally considered the way to become a Buddhist. People take refuge because they fear to be reborn again and again in states of woe. They consider that the Buddha found a way to freedom, taught the Dharma as that way and founded the Sangha, or community, that follows the way.

gTum-mo. The yoga of furor that generates a wrath-like energy usually from the navel center. This creates intense inner heat that is directed to melt down the nodes of awareness within the central nervous system and produce transformed states of realization. A side effect that has attracted interest in the West, most notably in the studies of Dr. Herbert Benson, is waves of heat radiating from the surface of the body.

Two truths. See Reality.

Ultimate nature. The ultimate nature of something is its real nature, the nature it will be found to have upon thorough investigation. It is opposed to a superficial nature, which something may seem to have but which cannot be found in that thing when it is subjected to scientific analysis.

Yoga. From the Sanskrit *yu,* 'to yoke', yoga is a discipline of yoking mind and body to the religious, philosophical or scientific quests of reality. General to all Indian schools, it implies the Indian insight that human beings may become what they know. Indeed it is a test for knowledge that valid knowledge will bear the test of experience and embodiment, while false knowledge will dissolve.

Select Bibliography

Alexander, F. *The Scope of Psychoanalysis*. New York: Basic Books, 1901.

Benson, H., Lehmann, J. W., Malhotra, M. S., Goldman, R. F., Hopkins, P. J., Epstein, M. D. 'Body Temperature Changes during the Practice of *gTum-mo* (heat) yoga.' *Nature* 295 (1982), pp. 234–6.

———. 'Body Temperature Changes During the Practice of *gTum-mo* yoga.' (Matters Arising) *Nature* 298 (1982), pp. 234–6.

———. *Beyond the Relaxation Response*. New York: Times Books, 1984.

———. *Your Maximum Mind*. New York: Times Books, 1987.

———. *The Relaxation Response*. New York: Morrow, 1975.

———, Malhotra, M. S., Goldman, R. F., Jacobs, G. D., Hopkins, P. J. 'Three Case Reports of the Metabolic and Electroencephalographic Changes During Advanced Buddhist Meditative Techniques.' *Behavioral Medicine* 16 (1990), pp. 90–5.

Brown, D. P. 'The Transformation of Consciousness.' *Noetic Sciences Review* (Spring 1988), p. 16.

Dalai Lama. *Freedom in Exile*. New York: HarperCollins, 1990.

———. *Kindness, Clarity and Insight*. Ithaca: Snow Lion, 1984.

———. *Opening the Eye of New Awareness*. Boston: Wisdom Publications, 1990.

———. *A Policy of Kindness*. Ithaca: Snow Lion, 1990.

David-Neel, A. *Magic and Mystery in Tibet*. New York: Penguin Books, 1971.

Dass, R. *How Can I Help?* New York: Knopf, 1985.

Dummer, T. *Tibetan Medicine*. London: Routledge, 1988.

Freud, S. *The Interpretation of Dreams*. New York: W. W. Norton, 1962.

———. *Civilization and Its Discontents*. New York: W. W. Norton, 1961.

Gardner, H. E. *Frames of Mind: The Theory of Multiple Intelligences*. New York: Basic Books, 1983.

————. *The Mind's New Science: A History of the Cognitive Revolution*. New York: Basic Books, 1985.

Goleman, D. *The Meditative Mind*. Los Angeles: Tarcher, 1988.

Gyatso, K. *Clear Light of Bliss*. London: Wisdom Publications, 1982.

Hopkins, J. *Meditation on Emptiness*. London: Wisdom Publications, 1983.

———— and Rinpoche, Lati. *Death, Intermediate State and Rebirth in Tibetan Buddhism*. Ithaca: Snow Lion Publications, 1979.

———— and Sopa, Geshe. *Cutting Through Appearances: Practice and Theory of Tibetan Buddhism*. Ithaca: Snow Lion Publications, 1989.

James, W. *Principles of Psychology*, 1910. Reprint, New York: Dover, 1950.

————. *The Varieties of Religious Experience*, New York: Crowell-Collier, 1961.

Jung, C. G. 'Psychology and Alchemy.' *Collected Works*, Vol. 12. Princeton: Princeton University Press, 1958.

Penrose, R. *The Emperor's New Mind*. New York: Oxford University Press, 1990.

Rabten, Geshe. *Mind and Its Functions*. Switzerland: Tharpa Choeling, 1979.

Rorty, R. *Philosophy and the Mirror of Nature*. Princeton: Princeton University Press, 1979.

Shantideva (trans. Batchelor). *Guide to the Bodhisattva's Way of Life*. Dharamsala: LTWA, 1979.

Thurman, R. A. F. *The Central Philosophy of Tibet*. Princeton: Princeton University Press, 1991.

Wangchen, Geshe N. *Awakening the Mind of Enlightenment*, London: Wisdom Publications, 1987.

Wilber, K., Engler, J. and Brown, D. P. *Transformations of Consciousness*, Boston: Shambhala, 1986.

Zimmer, H. *The Philosophies of India*. New York: Pantheon, 1951.

Index

The Sponsors

THE MIND/BODY MEDICAL INSTITUTE is a non-profit, scientific and educational organization dedicated to the study of Behavioral Medicine, including mind/body interactions and the relaxation response. Incorporated in October 1988, the Institute seeks to advance health and well-being by conducting basic and applied medical research, both independently and collaboratively; quantifying the cost benefits of mind/body and other Behavioral Medicine treatments; scientifically evaluating complementary healing practices including the role of belief; and disseminating the results of its findings through medical and general publications, lectures and symposia, and teaching and training programs. The Mind/Body Medical Institute is a subsidiary of NEDH Corp., the parent company of the New England Deaconess Hospital, and is affiliated with the Harvard Medical School. For information contact MIND/BODY MEDICAL INSTITUTE, 185 PILGRIM ROAD, BOSTON, MASSACHUSETTS 02215.

TIBET HOUSE in New York City is a non-profit, cultural and educational organization founded in 1987 under the auspices of His Holiness the Fourteenth Dalai Lama of Tibet. Through a wide range of art events, cultural programs and media outreach, it aims to help preserve Tibet's unique cultural heritage and to present to the West Tibet's ancient traditions of philosophy, art and science. For more information contact TIBET HOUSE, 241 EAST 32 STREET, NEW YORK, NY 10016.

The Publisher

WISDOM PUBLICATIONS is a publisher and distributor of books on Buddhism, Tibet and related East-West themes. Our titles are published in appreciation of Buddhism as a living philosophy and with the special commitment to preserve and transmit important works from all the major Buddhist traditions. Our East-West series was created to build bridges between the great philosophies, psychologies, sciences and arts of the world and to explore the universality of their ideas and methods. For more information, or a copy of our extensive mail order catalogue, please write to us at 361 NEWBURY STREET, BOSTON, MASSACHUSETTS 02115, USA.

Wisdom is a non-profit, charitable organization and a part of the Foundation for the Preservation of the Mahayana Tradition (FPMT).